Beauty Through It All
Barbara Jean Jeske

The Greatest Love to my Parents, My Father Arthur Elmer Jeske Jr. and My Mother Sylvia Gloria DeGroat Jeske. My Heart is with you both first. I miss you very much. The world and the Universe is a different place without you both. I can see and feel the difference.

# Table of Contents

# Chapter One

## But Why, and to Much

It was when I was very very young. I was at a neighbor's house, outside in the backyard playing. I went over to see what the other little kids were doing. When I got there, they were playing around some fire. My shirt caught on fire, and I ran as fast as my little legs could run. I ran fast to my house. I was screaming, my Mother was home. My Mother placed me in the bathtub, and turned the shower on me.The fire stopped, she placed a towel around me. Being very very young I can recall her loving me, and caring for me, to this day and in perpetuum. This point in time, only she, saved my life. I went to the hospital; I was there for some time. I recall laying on the hospital table and feeling the room very cold. The nurse said before she put a needle in my arm, she said I had good veins, that was gross. To this day that is nonsensical, and stupid to me. I had bandages on my body. I recall laying in a bathtub with warm water. The nurses peeling the bandages off of me.

The water helped the bandages come off better. I recalled at a very young age it smelled not so good. There was pain off and on.

My Mother came to the hospital to see me every day. My Father came to see me in the hospital, when he was not working. My Mother would bring me presents all the time. One of the presents she brought to me, were Danish troll dolls. One had black hair, one had orange hair, one had blonde hair and there were others. The bonding of my Mother, at that moment in time, was one of very importance for myself. For this was not any greatness of myself bonding to my Mother, but an importance of my healing of my body, mind, and spirit. Healing from my burns.

My Mother took me for a checkup on them, to this very old doctor. I was waiting with my Mother, even though my Mother was with me I did not want to be there. We waited in this small room. I went into another room to wait a little more. I sat at the bottom edge of a table with white covering on it. I was so very little in this moment of time. There was a large window with stained glass right in front of me. My body was shaking, for I was so scared. I looked around nothing was comforting me. The old doctor came in and he must've seen that I was shaking. Because he said, take this. He was giving me a white salted cracker. I looked at the cracker and thought I do not want this. I want something better. The whole building was very old. That is how it was then at the time. I did not want to go to the doctor, I just wanted to be at home, during these times. My Mother said we have to go someplace. So I got in the car. At that moment, I had to have another checkup. I got out of the car and ran with my little legs to the house. I screamed I am not going; I am not going. I screamed and wrapped my little arms, to part of the house. I screamed again. I cried so hard. By that time my Mother got out of the car, and she talked to me very gently. She said we will stop and get a treat of what I wanted. For myself this was the only, only way I was going to go. I really know this was hard for myself and my Mother to go through. We both needed a treat, I know even more than that. There were many times my Mother and I went to places to heal, what happened with the burns. My Mother was my best friend, my only friend, my true human being for myself. I deeply love her now and this is a lasting forever love. No one knew her as I did. I Thank you ever so very much Mother. When I was a very little girl, I did not know how to say, the word hospital. The word I said was hosberry, this sound good to myself. I think, I could of needed berries, for this sounds great also.

Where I was going to, was my Grandparents home in another town, passing this one big building I was thinking of this word hosberry. For a long period of time, I only knew the word hosberry. Until later in my life I found out the other way to say it. Hosberry still sounds great.

My Mother was absolutely there for me, and how she knew how to be there the way she did, that she did this herself. The love she had, and in this she was tremendously smart. Writing this I have some tears in my eyes. For the loving feelings for my Mother. I Thank my Mother for saving my life, and that I had her, to this day she is in myself. Throughout my life I healed myself, knowing what I went through with being so very young, and having fire on my body. Times were sometimes hard. But through any of it, there was my Father who was a man that I see as happy, and a gentleman in every way. Also who was, and is like myself. For all this is a strength, and a forever beauty that can be touched.

# Chapter Two

## The Greatest Gentleman in the World

My Father loved his sisters, and his brothers. My Father once said to me, blood is thicker than water. He communicated with his sisters, and his brothers. For he had an important closeness with his family. He came from growing up with them, in a farmhouse, out in the country, that his Grandfather, my Great-Grandfather had someone build for them. I once had a conversation with one of his brothers, my Uncle. I told my Uncle that my Father loved him, and my Uncle said that he missed my Father very much. I also had a conversation with one of his sisters, my Aunt. I told her that my Father loved her very much. She told me that she misses him very much. My Father is missed, ever so dearly, and loving missed. He is missed so much by me that it has hurt, and I needed to help it heal. I can heal myself, but missing my Father, this is a foreverness for myself. I know my Father, that I am like him, and that he has a presence in me, perpetually, and forever. He is with me right now. My Father, was and is now a Hero.

He was the President, of his own company, that he himself built up. He started when he was very young, working on vehicles, fixing them up, putting them back together. On the farm where he started his life, this was different for him than farming. Before he owned his own company he worked for a company that was in a very small building. I can recall where this small building was. I recall going with him, sometimes, just to look at it from the outside, the building was small. My Father was great at what he did, and he was proud of himself. He was a salesman, and I am going to say he was great.

Even though I was little, once I watched him, shine his shoes, and he then got all dressed up in a suit to go and sell. He became the best salesman I ever knew. For myself, this is exciting what he was doing, by getting all dressed up, to look great for his work. He was the most handsome man ever in the world. He won a lot of awards for selling, because he was so great at it. My Mother gave me some of his awards. I was so very little, when he had this job. This is in my blood, that I can make great deals as he did. But he is my Father, he is a man that I forever look up to, and forever know he is there, as I live my life. I am ever so proud of him, he is great. In my Father's office, I would hide, under his desk. This was fun for me. People that would work there, were walking around doing business. While I was under the desk, I could just see people's, shoes, and their legs, I heard them talking to each other, this was fun. I was so very young, when I hid under my Father's desk. I felt very protected under there, knowing that no one was going to bother me, no one knew I was there. My Father was the first man I knew of, who was my handsome Prince to me, and not anyone else. This is want makes me who I am right now, and the everlasting of myself. This is my world, and the world I once lived, and treasured. For this is in me, and for my life now. I am a princess for being born from two great people who are King, and Queen in my heart. My Father was a King, he was a King of my heart, and a real President. For my Mother, she was beautiful, and my Father was handsome.

I got a call from my Father. He told me that he bought a farm, and it had a house with it. My Father said, I could have anything in the house I wanted. I did say yes. I drove out in the country, and came to the driveway. I then drove to the house. There were people who worked for my Father doing things to the barn. I went over to the house. The house was next to some tall trees. I opened the door, and there was the kitchen. In the middle of the kitchen, there was a hole in the floor. The hole went to the basement. I looked around, there was so much stuff all around. I got a wooden table with wooden chairs. The table and chairs had about two or three layers of paint on them. I took them to a place where they take off paint, from any wood. The table and chairs turned out beautiful. My Father told me, the person who did the work of taking the paint off the chairs and table, they wanted to buy them from me. My Father thought this was great. But I was not going to sell them. The whole thing about these pieces, they were old, and good.

My Father was a very important man; bankers would come to him.

My Father, once drank from a china tea set, that was owned by Walt Disney himself, in his private office.

How sometimes it comes together, the beauty in me, and the beauty in my life. This all came together, before I was born, and after I was born. I think the talks with my Mother, that I told her this saying, so many times. She took this all in. I will forever, and forever say, and feel in my heart. I definitely know unquestionably, my Mother was so proud of me, and all I have done, and do. She told me so. At times now I will say how I miss my parents. Deep in my heart, I always had them both. They are both, in myself right at this moment. My parents, are in my heart, and I still miss each one. It is in my mind, and it goes into my heart. As a child, I always had this. I really know now that if, there was anyone else to love beside myself, unfathomably, my love goes to both of my parents. There was a connection then and now, and forever. For myself, I really, really miss them. If I could bring them back to life, I would do it loving, and greatly. For myself, I have really never connected to anyone when I was young. But this is what I love. Both of my parents had that uniqueness, I have in myself, I have seen in them. I am their child now, and I am their child then. They both knew, I am all who I am.

My Father, participated in tractor pulls. This is when someone is driving an antique tractor, that is pulling weights on the back of it. There is a competition, with other people to see how far down the track, they can go pulling the weights. There were a lot of people, in the grandstands, watching, and clapping their hands to cheer, the people driving the antique tractors. The prizes were money or trophies. One time my Father, entered one of his antique tractors, in a race. He drove it to the finish line, and he won the race. I came to watch him race. I was standing partly on the fence, outside of the area, where he was racing. Everyone was cheering. I came with him, and both him and I, went there together. When I was with him, the weather was very warm outside, it was summer time. I was just standing there, where I was watching him. He came over to me, and held out his hand, and handed to me, his winnings of the race, that he just won, first prize. I said with my feelings, and my thoughts, thank you. I wrapped my arms around him, and gave him a big hug, and a big kiss on his cheek. I am his oldest daughter, and I knew that he loved the whole thing. This was the kind of Gentleman, only my Father could be. I really forever, and for always loved him, and I miss my Father, all the time.

I drove a Massey Ferguson antique tractor, at tractor pulls, with my Father. I had my own antique tractor, my Father had me drive in the races. I raced the tractor, at a time when there were 25 men. I was the only woman in the group. I got 2nd place, out of 25 men. The person, that got first place was someone who wins a lot. When I was going down the track, and I was driving the antique tractor and about to finish pulling the weight with the tractor. There were some men cheering for me, on one side of me, when I was almost at the finish line. The men said, when I win, or get done, they were going to buy me a beer. As I was driving the tractor, and going to the finishing line to be done. I said to the men, I do not drink. Then the men said, back to me, they will drink for me. I just finished, to the end of the track, and I had a big smile, on my face, when I got to the finish line. I was overjoyed, because the men, knew I was in first place at that moment. That is why they wanted to celebrate, by buying me a beer. I did not know, I was in first place, at that moment in time. I could of won first place. But I was in first place, for a little while if that man who won first place that day, did not race, I could have won the race, I was told. The men on the sidelines, knew I was in first place, in that moment of time. I was just driving, the antique tractor, and just wanting to win. I was the only woman, that was there at the antique tractor pull competing. Yes, I won 2nd place, out of 25 men. What I won, was a trophy that was two and a half feet high. On top of the trophy, was a tractor five inches long. The little tractor on top, was made from some kind of hard metal. The wheels, on the little tractor moved around. I was so proud of myself having this trophy, and winning 2nd place, out of 25 men, and being the only woman there. The little tractor, on top of the trophy, was painted all green. Green is the color, for John Deere tractors. I can picture myself, driving the antique tractor in the race, and for myself just being on the tractor, and having the time of my life.

My Father, was there watching me. For he had to make sure, that the tractors, were working fine. My Father Loved doing tractor pulls. He loved antique tractors, because it brought him back, to when he grew up on his Father and Mother's farm. When I have told my Mother, this story at times about me winning 2nd place in the tractor pull, she loved it. She was proud of me, as she would say. She never had enough, of hearing the story. Her saying would be, yes, she won out of 25 men, and that is Barbara.

I know my Father was proud of me, he was right there. I have always known, my parents were always there, I mean just there as human beings. I have always known, that their homes, were my homes, if I needed a home. My Father was a very true man. His life was, and for myself, is a whole story and more. I was very much, like him. I looked like him more than anyone, I just did, and I am super glad, I do. My Mother told me a lot, I was like my Father. My Father was my rock, and looking at him now, there was not any gentleman more handsome then him. He was a very beautiful man, inside and out.

To know him you would be, very fortunate. I loved him, as if he was a super star. Well, in my book in my heart, and mind, he was my super star. I loved my Father then, and right now, forever and forever. I Thank You Father, for everything you give to me. I thank you, that you were my Father, then and now. My love goes to you, Father.

I was going almost everywhere my Father would go. If he said, he was going someplace, I was first to be in the car. I heard my Mother once say, she liked seeing this.

I recall, I was down stairs in the house that was in the city, I was sitting down on the floor making a patchwork quilt, as I was sewing the pieces together, my Father came over to me and sat down next to me. He started to talk to me and he said that his Mother, my Grandmother made quilts just like I was making. The togetherness at this very moment is priceless for myself. Years later, I was given my Grandmother's four wooden quilt boards, these were very old by the way they looked and they were used a lot by my Grandmother. I never used them, but I was going too.

My Father in his heart, was a genteel and sophisticated, and cultured man. The way he did things and who he is, in my heart, and he was real, and he was different than other people.

I once said to my Father, when he was driving in the car, and I was sitting in the backseat, I said to him, I do not want any inheritance, I want your love. He said to me, you have our love. This ride was in the countryside. Passing Spruce trees, that someone was growing in the area. My Father loved trees.

He once, went into his own woods, to find a tree I wanted. I stood on the outskirts of the woods, while he went to look for a tree for me. He came back, from looking in the woods a while, but he could not find a tree. My Father loved the woods, very much. The same time, I was by the woods with my Father, I seen a beaver dam, and trees cut down by the beavers. There was a creek, flowing so nicely, where it was going too. The beaver's teeth marks, were all over the bottom of the cut down trees.

I miss talking with my Father, and hearing his voice. Sometimes I stop to hear his voice. I miss letting him know I loved him. I miss taking walks with him, and just knowing he is close by me, for me to see him or talk to him. Yes, I am starting to cry, and tears want to come down my cheeks. I am trying to find the keys on the computer, because my eyes are getting watery.

# Chapter Three

## Too much pain, for any human being

After my Father died, there was a lot of pain. But after my Mother died, there were people that were around her, and not just anyone, but also professional people, that caused pain to me. My Mother, needed to pick better professional people. She was pressured, and so was my Father from people. I know for a fact. Pain I am healing from that, and to now. For I was the most precocious, and more pulchritudinous looking. I did not talk to a lot of people, for more than 20 years or more, that caused pain to me. They were around my Mother, at her death. The hate, that was around that moment in time, was way past the sky. I am saying this, ever so nicely, and very gently. This was very difficult. This story I could write about, but it is too long. There was so much negative. But I am a person who lives my life on, **optimistic breathing,** optimistic heart, soul, and mind. I am way so different to tell a story in my book, that does not need to be in it, at this point of time. The negative, was like swimming in it. People trying to put deep hurt to me, they could've remembered, my shirt caught on fire, and I had burns, when I was a very little girl.

One of the smartest, things that I could do, was just leave. I will never be around so much, negative people again. That much negative, can deeply hurt a human being, and cause harm. For I know how to be **optimistic** in the deepest part of my being. I know the strength of the mind,

and the heart. I know, peace that can wrap the heart, and
hug it, until the wound is healed, and the heart is calm. I
know what is better in life. For the worst of negative, I
could only save my mind, save my soul, save my body,
and I did. So now for myself, I am closer to my parents,
than ever before because of the beautiful safety net they
gave me, and their perpetually, and forever lasting love.
People having hurt put to me. They could've used their
minds or their hearts. What I am saying is they could think
a whole lot better than they did.
For myself, I stayed away from Birthdays, etc. Because I
wanted peace, and the greatness that peace has. I wanted
not any of the stress.
There was deep pain after my Mother died. What I am
going to say, how much hurt can humans do after my
Mother died. Any of the whatever's, happened after both of
my parents had died. Nothing bad as this, would have
happened if my parents were alive. My parents wanted
only good.
I am so, very rich for the fact, I do not act any different
before my parents, were alive or after they died. For I can
live in greatness of every kind, and greatness of every
color of the rainbow, and more. I was in the car, with my
parents once, and I said to them, I want the gold at the end
of the rainbow. For there was a rainbow in the sky at that
point.
I love them both, deeply and forever.
There were times I cried day and night. I woke up sitting on
the bed crying. There was hurtful pain. I cried when I was
talking to someone in Europe. I cried a lot. Through my
crying, and talking to friends I knew, they listened, and they
cared. I really knew they cared. I got a lot of strong hugs.
For these people are gentle people, when they hugged

me, they were strong. I was given wisdom to, in this I really needed.

So many things of hurting, were **power plays** from people. I know, that there is love, and that should of been a lot stronger, than anything. For my own Mother, had a sign saying, life is fragile handle with care. I would see this sign, a lot in her house. I say, Love can be a strength stronger than anything in the world. First, there is love, and everything can follow from that. I know this for a fact. I can look back, and see I am right totally now. I was once, sitting in my parent's living room. My Father, said to my Mother, Barbara is right. For I did not know all the conversation they were talking about. But just having them say, I am right on something was grand, for me. There were some people when I was young, that showed more feelings, and some did not show feelings at all. I was not like that, and never understood it. For myself I do both, I do my mind, and my feelings every minute.

I healed myself, through this bad. I listened to inside myself, and I guided myself, and there were good people I talked too. For they all knew what I was talking about. For there was over the top, too much my body did not need from people that were not good to me. For it could've been much nicer, for both my parents when they were alive, and myself now. I know how to be great, and I am very smart, I know how to be a real professional. Thank you Father, for gifting this to me.

# Chapter Four

## Breathtaking air outside

The pain my body had, was hurting too much. I know I really needed, fresh crisp clean outside air to breathe, in my body. For my body connects to the trees, the ground, the air, the sky, and Mother nature. I walk every place I go. I can take a plane or train, or drive. My place is to walk. I have walked up the hills, and parts of mountains in Switzerland, and towns to other towns. From one place to another, I have walked. I have walked from one country, to the next country next to it. I can speak some Schweizerdeutsch, and I am learning more. I have lived in Switzerland for a long, length of time. By my walking, I touched, and felt the ground, I smell the air outside, I can be next to the trees. For this, there is an openness of my being, for the pain, I have gone through, there has been years of it. Before I slept at night, I would start sweating. The sweat, was dripping. Dripping all over myself, and dripping sweat from my head too. This went on for 2 to 3 hours. Then I threw up, about 4 times, sometimes more. This was before, I went to bed to sleep, or when I woke up in the morning. But through the years now, it has gotten better. The stress, I have been around, was a large negative, I did not need it on my body. The stress, was as if it was swimming around myself. It was negative people, that I got away from. For myself, I have always wanted to be away from any bad.

I have left, and I have been away from a lot of negative,
that I never have asked for, not ever. But for myself, I am
not next to it, or an ear from it.
I have a free spirit, and that is who I am, and now I am
really free for myself, and I can create my life as I did
before, but there were negatives, this is nicely saying it,
negatives.

# Chapter Five

## Getting my Hearts Desires

When I was growing up, on my Father's side of the family, they lived without television, and lived somewhat like the Amish do. My Mother's side of the family watched television, and lived as anyone did. For myself, I was wearing new clothes all the time. I recall one of the very first Christmas that I had, my Mother said for me to, pick any 3 items in the Sears, or Jcpenney Christmas catalog that I wanted, and I can have it. I picked out what I wanted, every year after that one. It was so much fun picking anything I wanted in the catalogs. I recall, when the catalogs came, I would open them with great happiness, opening first the front cover, then pages in the catalog, to see what I wanted. I sometimes took the page out of the catalog, to save it until I got it. I recall, once I was so overjoyed, because I wanted a vanity table, and chair set. I had seen it in the catalog, and there it was, in the living room, wanting for me. I was so very little, but my arms were going to pick this up. I picked up the vanity table, and chair with my little arms, and carried it to my bedroom. I stood and I just looked, how beautiful this was. Thinking of this now, it was a very beautiful set, the color was white, and on top in the middle, it had a mirror, there was four thin legs to hold it up. This was all mine.
Going on trips, and living a different life than my Mother's side of the family, or my Father's side of the family. Sometimes it was really different for me, when there were

family gatherings. I would be looking really different than any of them. For myself, this was my way of life, and all that I was, and all that I am, the same now. I even felt different, all the time. For this is being just myself, and a world of dreams, that I was living really, that could be called a dream life, and this world that was all mine. I loved it so much. Looking at this now, I am very, very proud of myself, and my life then, and now. This gave to me, all that I am today. I know at times, with both of my parents coming from two totally different families. This was very hard on my parents at times. Being young, I seen it, and felt it. But my parents stayed together, and made their way of life. Both of my parents, were great people, they were very different than anyone. I was very much a part of the making of this life, I was there, and I see it. For myself, it was a movie, and I was on a movie set. For this was the greatest of all, but this was home life, mixed with business. Any of the stress of this, could have separated my parents, and it did not. For myself, I stayed all that I am, and more. There was pain, but healing is much better.

Whenever I have talked with people, if it is in Switzerland, England, Austria, or in Scandinavia, I speak some of their language, and I speak English. I speak some Swedish and I am learning more. I lived in Sweden for some time, I lived in England for a long time too. I have been at many, many castles, throughout Europe, and I lived in some for a while, and I felt right at home.

I had to say if anything about family. I would say, my family was like the television show Dallas. How the actors, played a strong family, and faked loving each other. Really not liking each other. To going against each other, for the power of money, or any other kind of power. And how I seen, and heard, and felt it all. How I seen, and felt the power plays in my life. I love power but, not in the terms of hate, and negative feelings. When I was growing up, my Father, was the President of his very own company, a company that he worked so hard at, and there were stresses after stresses, he went through. He made it happen for himself, and his family. I am feeling this hard now, because I am so proud of him, and all the greatness, he gladly gave me, in his heart, and for himself. This gentleman, is my dear, Father.

I grew up, different than other people, I can notice the difference, every moment of my being, and my wonderful life. I grew up, with different dates, years, places of times, then it is now. The places, were a lot better, the times, were more magical, and dates of the year were more creative. Plus, a person, would want to live that way.

I know when things, became very hurtful in my life, my parents were not there. I had to save my own self, and I saved my own soul.

Sometimes I just see my parents, and for myself, this is everything.

The power of anything, the hugs, and saying I love you, sometimes just got in the way.

I lived at times for myself, I was only psychological, and philosophical with communication, at times with anyone. There were times, negative people wanted to control, if it was for one reason or another. The power was high for them, again whatever the power was.

For a saying my Father told me. My Father and I were walking in his backyard. We were walking, to his home. The air was clear, and it was beautiful out, the birds were singing their songs, the trees smelled really good. My Father said, blood is thicker than water. He just came out, and said it to me. I had no way of why he said it, at that time, and place. But months, and years from that, I know

now. For positive energy, wins out every time. The negative energy, goes away far in the wind.

I was out riding in the car with both my parents, as we did a lot. My Father, was driving along a lake. On each side of the road, there were trees, we were in the woods. But still, the lake was very close. My Father stopped, and I do not recall that there was a for sale sign or not. But he turned right, onto a small road, leading to a small old house. In front of the small little wooden house, it had a little open porch. Just a few steps, from the open porch, there was the lake. There was no one home. My Father got out of the car, then I got out. My Mother stayed in the car. I followed my Father to the house, he looked around the house. I went to the shore of the lake. The water at the shore was clear, as I was looking at the water, I seen very large salmon fish. My eyes were like, seeing the biggest fish ever. The fish were swimming so beautifully, and they looked beautiful.

My Father, did not buy this small lake front house. But this is, something he would do. He bought, and sold, this was his love, to do, and his love of business, for he was a farmer first in his heart, then at the same part, he was a **Magnificent, and Brilliant** business gentleman.

# Chapter Six

## Living like a Royal

I entered through very tall, and wide wooden, ostentatious doors. I placed first, one step then the other step, into the magical palace. There were opulent paintings, high above on the ceilings. There were chandeliers in rows, on each side of the walkway, in my presence. I kept walking until the middle of the big room. For I have heard tales, of Kings, and Queens, being married here. As I walked more, I could feel royalty right with me, and I was the royal too.
I was there, when a lady became a Princess, after she married the countries Prince. I was one of the first people in the world, to see them when they were first married, His Royal Highness Prince and Her Royal Highness Princess in person.
After the wedding, they went in the open carriage, with beautiful grand looking horses pulling it. The carriage was an open carriage, with antique glass lights in the front of it. There were footmen, riding on the open carriage, and coach men in front of the open carriage, holding on to the reins of the horses, directing the horses were to go. On the side of the open carriage, was a gold painted crown. After His Royal Highness Prince, and Her Royal Highness Princess got into the open carriage, the open carriage with both of them in it, went out of the large wooden doors, of the palace. The open carriage with His Royal Highness Prince, and Her Royal Highness Princess, came down a

small hill on the side of the Palace. Then the open carriage turned left, to go in front of the Grand Palace. On this very magical moment, I seen His Royal Highness Prince, and Her Royal Highness Princess in the open carriage. First I seen the horses, there were a lot of horses pulling the open carriage. The horse's legs, were moving at a good pace. The horses were very beautiful and tall, they were taken care of very well, they shined in the sun. I was right next to them, I could have touched the horses, and the horses smelt good. Then the open carriage was right in front of me. I see the coach men, then I see right in front of myself, His Royal Highness Prince with his military outfit on, he was smiling, and looking straight ahead. At that second moment, I seen the sun shining on the emeralds, that were placed on top of the diamonds, as part of the decoration, on the tiara, that Her Royal Highness Princess was wearing. His Royal Highness Prince, and Her Royal Highness Princess sat nicely in the open carriage. Both of these two royals were just a touch of a hand away from me, I was right next to them, and I see their faces. The sun was shining ever so brightly. The open carriage left down the street for a while, then came back, to the palace.
In front of the Grand Palace, there was a garden with green grass, and walkways in the grass. There were beautiful flowers set in different places, the flowers put a smile on the faces of the people looking at them. There were urns, placed in the garden, to the touch of the royal living. In the garden, I saw a beautiful, Her Majesty the Queen, wearing a red gown and she had a tiara on her head with brightly sparkling diamonds, I knew the wonderful country Her Majesty the Queen was from. Then I see another beautiful, Her Majesty the Queen, wearing a yellow gown and she had a tiara on her head, with brightly sparkling diamonds on it, I also knew the wonderful country

Her Majesty the Queen was from. Another beautiful, Her Majesty the Queen, that was there, wore a tiara, that had amethysts and diamonds to decorate the tiara, I knew the wonderful country Her Majesty the Queen come from. I see a beautiful, Her Majesty the Queen, wearing a burgundy color lace gown, her hair was very beautiful, it was twisted in a bun in the back of her head, I knew the wonderful country, Her Majesty the Queen was from.

I see Her Royal Highness Crown Princess, wearing a tiara with beautiful diamonds that sparkled in the sun, and her hair is beautiful, some of her hair was wrapped around parts of her beautiful tiara. There were two beautiful, Her Royal Highness Princesses, wearing light blue gowns, with diamond tiaras. There was a beautiful, Her Royal Highness Crown Princess, wearing a medium color blue gown, with a diamond tiara. I see two beautiful, Her Royal Highness Princesses, wearing pink gowns, with diamond tiaras. One Her Royal Highness Princess, had ostentatious, exquisite pink earrings with diamonds, and Her Royal Highness Princess that was wearing a pink gown, with the ostentatious, exquisite pink earrings with diamonds, was smiling with great happiness, I knew the wonderful country she came from. The men that were there, wore their military uniforms, and some wore greatly designed tailored suits, they would of been His Royal Highness Crown Prince, or His Royal Highness Prince, or other Gentlemen, I seen His Majesty the king, and all the men were handsome. His Majesty the King was there, who loved his wonderful country with the greatness of honor, I also knew the wonderful country he came from.

There in the garden, were also a lot of His Royal Highness Crown Princes, and Her Royal Highness Crown Princesses, and Princes, and Princesses and they wore ostentatious tiaras with diamonds, and the tiaras were

decorated most ornately, and beautifully designed. I knew the countries, His Royal Highness Crown Princes, and Her Royal Highness Crown Princesses were from, and they were walking and taking in the garden. One special Her Royal Highness Crown Princess was wearing white, with a little bit of soft grays on her gown, it was flowing beautifully in the wind. She had a tiara on, with diamonds that circled around for the decoration, on the tiara. Her handsome His Royal Highness Prince, was right next to her, and he was a gentleman in every way. Both of them had smiles that showed their forever deep love, for each other.
There were other Ladies who were at the Royal Palace garden, they were talking to each other, and they were also wearing tiaras, and there were other Gentlemen who were looking aristocratic, and pulchritudinous. Their faces were happy, and they were all glad to be there. The diamonds on the ladies' tiaras, caught the rays of the sun, and the tiaras shined ever so brightly, brilliantly and Breathtakingly, beautiful.
Was this a dream, could of this, been a dream. Did I want, this to be a dream, this all really happened. This is what I dream anyways. I was here, I seen every part of this magical life.

I said hello, to a beautiful little Her Royal Highness Princess, who could someday be an exquisite beautiful Her Majesty the Queen. She has a smile that lights up the world, and a face that has my heart melt. I said hello to her, when she was riding in the Royal open carriage. I am glad I seen her, and she saw me. Dreaming this one day, or was it just a thought, no not at all, this was very real, I waved and said hello to her.
For my life has been, somewhat like the Royals I seen. My Father was the President of his own Company, and I am

his Daughter. I feel this is ever so much now, of who I am. I was living it ever so much then. But the now, has myself just as if I was young, living it then, for it is my life right now, and forever always, this makes it all what I am. I lived like a princess, growing up. I am glad I have my life, this has made me a Grand Lady, and a Queen in my Heart.

# Chapter Seven

## Being Loved so very much, richly

There was a Lady, who I have talked with, who lives in Europe. She once said to me, only 1% of the population of the world could have done the things, or at that time and place, gone through what I have. I am saying this; the hardness was too much for any human.

My Mother, and I were at a dress shop, by a town where my parents had a cottage, a house on the lake. The shop was down the street, were my Father, was getting his boat fixed. My Mother and I, were looking around in the shop. We were in the shop a while, my Mother said to me, I could pick out anything in here I wanted. I thought wow, and I said yes. Before going in the shop, I thought my Mother was going to look for something just for her. I looked around the nice dress shop, and I found something for myself, we were just both happy to be in the shop that day. Maybe because it was nice to be in town, instead of at the cottage. We checked out, and left. We then went over to where my Father was getting his boat fixed. My Father did get his boat fixed. I like both the city, and the country.

I grew Edelweiss, in the city. This is a flower of the European alps, and it grows wild in the Alps.

When that happened with the fire with me, as in Chapter One, after I came home with my parents. I was always missing the shirt I was wearing, when the fire happened. When I was very little, I would think about it all the time, and wonder what happened to the shirt. This took a very long time, of thinking about, what happened to my shirt. Not until I was way older, I could only understand what happen to the shirt I liked, and it was mine. The shirt, was orange colored, with a lion in front. How I really wondered, and then in time the not knowing, came completely together. The fire was, on the shirt that I liked. Then it was gone. I am glad to be alive.

My Father, did his own company great. I also have learned from him, wonderful, and great things.

Once my Father, married my Mother, he changed from how his family did some things. So for myself growing up there was a group of family that lived one way, then the other. But in my parent's marriage, they both had a lot of stress with how their families were so very different, it was not easy for them. For my parents, raising children, developing my Father's company, and having their families they came from, was not easy at moments in time.

My Mother, once had a needle point saying, that hung on the wall, and nicely framed. The saying said, Life is fragile, handle with care. I do not know if she needlepointed it herself, or not. But this saying is sweet.

My Grandmother, made the best rice krispies bars than anyone, she lovingly made them for me to eat. She made a whole big pan full. I would come over to her house in the city. I would walk up the wooden stairs, then step on the wooden porch. She had a wooden swing on her porch. I came through the door into the living room, there she would be at times, if she was not in her kitchen. She would be holding the pan of rice krispies bars that she just made. She was the best cook, she made everything by hand. My Grandmother made the greatest pies, cookies, and lunch, and supper, everything was so delectable. I was in her kitchen, watching her all the time, or I would be making food of all kinds with her. When I came over, at times I came in her house in the side door. When I did, I would open the door, and start walking up the narrow, small wooden stairs, that would bring me right up to the kitchen. This very moment walking up the stairs, I always either smelled her great cooking, or wondered what she is making in the kitchen. For myself, it was always a wonder, a feeling of bewilderment. I love my Grandmother, on my Mother's side of her family. But I loved, both of my Grandparents on my Father's side of his family very much also.

Once I seen a wooden playhouse, tall enough for myself to walk in when I was very young. This playhouse, was at my Aunt's house on the side of their house. It was painted red, and white. The Aunt was on my Father's side of the family, his sister. One day, something was being built in the backyard, of my house. The playhouse, that I saw was being built. This was so good.

I recall, I had a lot of dreams when I was very young, dreams that were for myself, I thought were real. I would dream that I was flying, and I woke up thinking I really was flying. For myself, this became so real, and this meant I would fly. I have flown on airplanes, at a very young age and older, I have flown almost around the world. Parts of the world, I feel very close too. Sometimes I feel, that I have lived on a plane.

For years, and part of my life, I helped her, so greatly, my Mother, I just burned out, too many times, because people around her stress was a life for them, not me. I did not see my Mother for about a year, before she died, because the hurt and living just on the way with them, psychological, or

philosophical was just not everything, I am. Both my
parents only, really knew all that I am.

My Father, who I received a lot of Love from, and a power
of good strength, gives myself the ability, to be more of all I
am, and more. My Father once said to me, do something
that I love, that is in my heart.

I would be at my Mother's house, I would ask her what she
wanted to eat, that she had in her house. She said to me
what is your heart's desire. At that moment in time, I
thought what does she mean with that. Now I know.

When my Mother was still in the hospital, at this point, the
last time, before she went home. I went back to see her,
she said where is Barbara, where did she go. I was out in
the hall, I told her. When I was next to her in the room that
she was in, she said to me, I would like to go shopping to
buy you a new skirt. I did not say anything to her, for by her
saying this to me, this was something that made her feel
better. The skirt, I was wearing was white, and had lace cut
out hearts on the bottom, the skirt I bought new. I still have
this skirt, and I love it. The coat I was wearing, was felted
wool, the buttons were made from deer antlers, and there
was Austrian stitching on parts of it. I bought this in Austria.
I loved the coat, this coat was a coat a man would wear.
Both my Mother, and myself loved shopping so much in
our lives. Right now, saying any of this I really miss her so
fervidly, and I am ready to have tears come rolling down
my cheeks.

My Grandfather, on my Mother's side of the family was
Brothertown Indian. He had a violin that he loved to play.
He played his violin at barn dances, in different towns, for a
lot of years, plus where he could play, he loved it. I can just
think of myself, being there watching him play. Hearing the
music, from the violin. He was a very good gentleman. He

was a good husband to my Grandmother. My Grandmother talked about him. I would have loved to have his violin. I bought a violin at an auction. I play some violin. For myself, violin is one of the best sounds to hear, and to tap my feet too.

# Chapter Eight

## Story of light, in the Heart

My Great Grandparents had to move out fast, or they were forced to move. One time in my life, I had almost something like the same thing as my Great Grandparents, went through. My Great Grandparents and I, had it the same way about, I am better now, for I left. I feel close to my Great Grandfather, for what he went through, because his strength, and love I knew was in me, for I am a part of him. I knew some of what he went through. We both had a connection. With myself, knowing how he would have felt, all this gives me a strength I need. I felt my Great Grandfather smiling at me, and putting his arms around me at many points in times. For I had no one else, but he was there in my heart, and I just knew this. I Thank you, Great Grandfather, and Great Grandmother she was with me also, and I thank her and we are together. I am ever so proud of this, and I am a lucky lady.

My Mother once said to me, what can you not do, I was just thinking, I can do everything, this felt good.

Even if I did not see my Mother, for about a year before she died, in that time I know she had love for me, and we were close. This was hard, on myself, but I stayed away from people's stress. That would have put hardness on me. But I know a Mother's love is a love that never goes away, and it is connected stronger, tighter than most, anything in the world.

My inside was pain after pain at one point in time. I could
of, if I could just reach inside of myself, with my hands, and
stopped the pain. This did heal from pain, but I always will
know of this, by just for myself, getting smarter at it all.
My Father was in Panama, at one time in his life. He asked
my Mother, if she would move there with him, she said no.
I know that they should have. They would of had even a
better life than they had, this could've been something they
should have tried. I always told them that they should
move away.
There was a jacket, that my Father had that I liked, I had it
after him. He said, I liked the jacket because he wore it.
For myself, it was because he wore it, and I just liked it. My
Father one time called my Mother, to tell me to pick him up
at work. I went over to do it. In the car my Father said to
me if he sold the business, the people would not have
work. I do not know why he said this, but he knew why he
said it. I was just very glad to get the call to pick him up at
his company.
I could of had my Father's whole Company, I knew the
work he put into it. I knew what he went through to have it.
I was there when so much was happening. I recall, so
many, many times I waited in the car when he went to
another company, to just talk to them about business, he
went a lot. He worked like no one I have seen work. I can
see myself, working to much like him at times. People were
hard on him at times, he did not ever need that. He was a
man that gave more than anyone I ever knew. Plus, there
were people around him, that I was never going to do
business with. I did not want, the company, because it was
only his company, and no one could ever be him, or do
what he did with his company. For what he did, not a single
person could ever do, or have. For myself, I got from my
Father, what he did for me, or what he gave to me, no one

else ever could do as he did. What my Mother, did for me not anyone could do what this beautiful lady did for me. I am their oldest daughter, and I am like both of my parents. I have my Mother; she gave me life. I love them both, forever.

I had a Birthday party, for my Mother. I called her sisters, and other people to come. It was a surprise. I had it at a restaurant, in a different town than where she lived. This restaurant was decorated from the 1950s. The food was good, and they had good healthy choices, and everything was homemade, just what my Mother liked. Even the muffins, and cakes, and cookies were homemade. I had a very special handmade designed cake, made for her to be delivered to the restaurant. So everyone needed to go there, and when she got there she would be surprised. This town that the party was in, there was a small lake right next to it. The party was great, and she was overjoyed. I could not go because, I had to work.

I had a birthday party for myself, this was an hour and a half away from where I lived at that time. My Mother was there, we ate at an Italian restaurant, that made fried ravioli, with parmesan cheese on top, this was so delicious. There was a small lake next to the restaurant, that I could see out the window, when I ate. I opened a present, and it was a CD of a wonderful singer. I was happy to get it. My Mother was watching me, and she wanted the CD also, because she loved music and she knew that if I liked this singer she would like it also. Music was a love of hers. After all this, we took a walk around the lake. My Mother was always so proud, that she walked a lot when she was young, to places she wanted to go too. The house where I lived in town, my Father was taking a drive in the downtown area. Before he went past this very big department store, he would slow down. The reason for slowing down so much, the fact was in the big window of the department store, there were stuffed little chipmunks, dancing around, and singing to their heart's content. So my Father slowed down, as long as he could, because there were cars lined up behind him. I was happy when he could stop longer, the department store was on a corner with, stop and go lights. So when the lights were red I got to hear the chipmunks sing, and dance longer. This was so cute, and fun. I was so very little, in this most beautiful moment in time, of my life.

My Father asked me, if I would go with him to the travel agent with him. I said ok, so off we went. We got there, and we all sat down, I was told that I could go anyplace I wanted. I said Hollywood, California. Then the question was answered. I went with the family. The reason I said Hollywood, California was I wanted to be a movie star. Not one person ever knew of this, the family did not talk much to each other on things. Going to California, I was going to ride some horses, I asked my Mother to ride, but she just said no. I did not understand why she did not want to ride a horse. But along time after that I realized that she was born in the city, and so was I. But with myself, I love both the city, and the country. This was fine that she did not ride. I rode a horse on paths in the hills. The horse I rode would not want to go over a stream of water. Someone had to take my reins, and pull the horse over the stream.

Later in life my Father moved my Mother out to the country, from the city. My Mother did not like it for a long time. I heard about this for a while, from her. But after she had a good home with my Father, she then was happy for her new home. She did not leave.

When I was little, I went with my Father to a big store in the downtown, city area. He went to this store because, he got his company's name embroidered on his coats, he wore, and other people wore them too. While he was in the store doing this, I got to look around. They had jewelry boxes made, as if they were little Austrian farmhouses. When I saw these for the very first time in my young life, I felt like these are my homes, and I wanted to own one. But these were small, but this did not matter I wanted to live in them. This was a special thought I had, the first time I seen the Austrian farmhouses, that were jewelry boxes, I wanted a home from them. My thoughts about these came so very true. I lived in Austria for a length of time. I lived in different homes, and castles in Austria at times, as these little jewelry boxes looked like. I see the inside of these homes, I smelt the home cooking, then I ate the cooked food. I talked the Austrian language to the people who owned the homes, or castles. For myself, to this very day these people are considered my closest family, and friends forever more. I am thanking Austria for this. For myself, this started with going with my Father to the big department store, and falling in love with, the little Austrian homes. And starting a dream that, came true, that is really there. This is my whole life in a circle, to seeing it, to having it in my heart, and living my whole life with my dream, or my dreams are myself. To the jewelry boxes that were small, to these Austrian farmhouses, bigger than myself now, I completed the circle with a touch of my eyes.

When I was so young, the house in town where I lived, was a house I loved living in. Once in a moment in time, on a very nice sun shining day, the very first time I made money, was from glass pop bottles that were empty in the garage. I got some, and I walked through the back door, then I went in the backyard. Down the sidewalk, to a little store that I could get money back for the bottles. Way back in time, when pop came only in glass bottles. I got a little amount of coins for taking the bottles back. I bought some little pieces of candy that cost 2 cents, for each piece. This was all, important for myself.

# Chapter Nine

## Happiness, in my Heart

When I was very young, my Father knew I loved horses. He once asked me if I wanted one, and I said yes. One day he took off, from his work, that he was the President of his own company, and he could take off when he wanted too. We got in the car, and he drove me to someone's house, we got out of the car, and the house was big, and beautiful. The owner of the house asked us to come in. I came in and when I opened the door to step in, there was a staircase shaped beautifully, as I looked at it, the staircase, went upward in a curve. There was a beautiful, ostentatious chandelier, right next to the staircase. The chandelier, had a special shine to the staircase, right next to it, they were both, beautifully designed. We walked in the backyard, where the grass was leading to a barn. When I got closer to the barn, I was so delighted to see horses. I was thinking, this is the best. I looked for the horse, that was for sale, it was an appaloosa horse. The horse was very beautiful, with nice spots. I was asked if I wanted to take the horse for a ride, I said no, the people who owned the horse, had an inside arena that they did things with horses, as I looked at the horse, there was no connection with myself to the horse. So my Father, did not buy it. But going with my Father was really great, to do this with him, to do it together. Another time, I went with my Father to look for a horse, and to see if it was the one I wanted. Someone was selling a horse in the backyard of their house it was a pretty pinto horse. This was not the right horse for me.

I am proud of my last name, I love the fact that it is all mine, I will take it forever, and ever with me, with the greatest of pride.

I have been into a store when I was very young, that always had me feel happy. I would open the old wooden door, and as soon as the door opened, a bell would ring. I then stepped into the store, as I stepped, there was a wooden floor, that was beautifully, old. As I took another step on the floor, the floor in some parts were squeaking. To this very day I love this floor, I was so very little, and this for me was something very new, and the first time for me being in a toy store. There were dolls on the highest shelf, dressed in clothes from different countries around the world. For myself, the dolls were the most beautiful things that I ever seen. I would look at one, and turn around, then turn around again, and see so many different kinds of dresses on so many dolls. I know, my mind just touched magic. As I walked around the store, there were tables right next to the walls all made of wood, that had things to buy, for children, to play with. They also sold other things, as fabric etc. Being a child all I cared about was anything I wanted to have, and that would be fun to play with. The dolls that were on the top shelf, I would dream of going to the places, and the countries, that each of the dolls dresses were made from, different countries. For myself, I was there in different countries, I lived in different countries and seen ladies wearing dresses, as the dolls I once looked at, when I was so very little. I have been in their homes, I ate with them, and spoke their own language, with them. I lived in their home, for a while. I lived, and dressed the way they did, and some more of their cultures, at times, I did. This is a real thing, mixed with dream, and equaled together. For the dolls can be real people, they are there, in sight, and in mind, or as I lived it, they're so very real. I can be one of those dolls now, for it is how I live, and for myself, I lived it.

I went to a furniture shop with my Father. The shop was in the city, in the downtown area. It was on the 6th floor of the building. There was a lot of different kinds of furniture. I was standing there next to my Father; he was talking to a man a lot. My Father did a lot of talking to people, and by this he did a lot of deal making. He was a great business man; he was the best. He did great deals. I was very little at this moment of time. At the furniture store, at one point my Father stopped talking with the man. My Father turned to me, and said pick out any bedroom set I wanted. I picked out one, that was white with gold painted ornate design. This was a French provincial style, bedroom set. For to this very day, I did not know how good my Father did at making great deals, when I was very young. But now, I can do great deals, as he always did. For he was a gentleman, that I loved, and he was there to keep me safe, in my life when I was little, and for me, he will always keep me safe. For now, I know the great way of buying and selling, because of being next to my Father when he did it, my Father was a natural at it, and I am also. He made so my deals. He would be, the man on the moon, or on the stars looking down upon me, being ever so proud of me. I have happiness in my Heart.

# Chapter Ten

## Fishing, and my horses

At the cottage, I drove snowmobiles all over, and places around the lake, and to the other lake next door. I drove mini bikes, they were called that, but they were very small motorcycles. I drove them to get to place to place.

I water skied with two skies, then I did one ski, I water skied with one ski, all the time after that. Then I tried to go barefoot water skiing. I stayed with using just one ski, to water ski. I was great at water skiing, with one ski. I went over the waves, with sheer delight. When the water was calm, for myself this was relaxation to just, water ski with the blue of the water, and the smoothness, of my ski going on the water, as it just glided along, as far as I wanted it too.

I went on the sailboat myself, and how I felt peaceful, and happy with the water all around myself, and the soft cool or warm air of the woods, together mixing with the water. I touch the water with my feet or hands, there is a clean fresh feel, I did not want to stop touching the water. For this put moisture in my skin, and my skin never forgot about this. My eyes never forgot, about my moments of my life, on the water, that I loved so very much.

I drove, what is called a boat that had a motor on the back of the boat. I drove this a lot. I took the boat out a lot to go fishing by myself. This was just myself, and the boat, the water, and the woods. I caught a lot of fish, I caught bluegill fish, sunfish, small and largemouth bass fish, northern pike fish, and perch fish. When I caught the fish, I cleaned them, and cooked them. I got to enjoy my fishing even more.

I was once in Canada. I went fishing right next to a lake with very clear water. At one part of the lake, there were rocks, high enough that I had to walk a little to be on top of them to fish. There were tall, blue and green Spruce trees, all around on each side of the rocks. There was a waterfall, coming down ever so gently, and softly, flowing with a small amount of water. The water had colors of white, and soft medium blue colors. The sound of the waterfall, was calming and relaxing, and it felt fresh in the air, I breathed in the air and for myself, there was peace in this place to behold in my heart, and mind. I was fishing with two men on each side of me. I cast out my fishing line, and I was fishing for a while, by the time I was done fishing, I caught 13 fish, and the men that were next to me caught none. Happy I was, happy the fish liked my bait. I cleaned the fish, with a greatness of pride. The fish were so white, and fresh, and very clean tasting. I can fish.

I swim, and when I swim, I swim very good, I swim like a fish.


For there was a little store down the road from the cottage. They sold some food items, candy, ice cream, and gas and etc. I would go there to buy gas for my mini bike, it was like a little motorcycle.

My Father bought a farm by the cottage. The farm was just a little bit away, just down the road from the cottage. In one of the barns there was space, where my horse could live. The barn had land next to it, opened land, and then the woods. I took the mini bike, from the cottage to were my horse was. I opened the wooden door, and I see my horse standing there and eating, as my horse was eating, it stops eating, and it lifts up its head to look at me. I go over to my horse and I lift up one leg, then I go to the hoof of the horse, so I can check the bottom of it, and clean it out, then I do anything else what I need to do before I put the saddle on my horse. I got on my horse, and I would ride through the wide field, with the wild flowers growing wild all over the field. I recall a beautiful glow of light, beaming all round my horse and I as we started entering the woods. I proceeded, to enter the woods, with my horse's hooves, crunching the leaves on the floor of the woods. Moving between, the small trees, and the big trees. I could inhale the woods, of its woody smell, and the trees with their ever so different kinds of leaves. The wind that was passing in the air throughout the woods, made it comforting for my horse, and myself. We both liked going in the woods, and my horse loved running through the field, with the wild flowers, growing ever so beautifully in the grass.

I rode my horse, to a small road that took me to the cottages, I did this often.

I also had a horse out in the country, somewhere else other than by the cottage. At this point in time, there was a place where people watched out for other people's horses. This is called boarding a horse. Before I rode my horse, as I always did, I cleaned my horse hooves, then brushed the horse, and etc. then put the saddle on. I then put my foot into the stirrup, and lifted myself up, and pulled my other leg up, and then around the back top of my horse, over to the other side of my horse, then sat on my horse to ride. The smell of my horse was always very nice. The bond, was always, strong and beautiful, I am going to call it ostentatious. These were my horses, and I knew how I felt with them, and the friendship I had with them.

I am part Native American Indian, and I really feel it when I am on a horse, or when I do a lot of things in my life.

One point in time, I started to ride, on the side of a country road, as I did many, many times. I rode a few miles to a woods, and then turned back to where my horse was boarded. Many times on beautiful sunny days, I would take the same way riding my horse. I would go passed a small farm that had a horse in front of their house, right next to the road. The horse would come as close as it could, to my horse and I, but there was a fence that stopped the horse from coming any closer to us. I could feel that the horse just wanted to be free. When I would go passed, riding my horse, the other horse would see my horse, and started to make a horse's noise, out of its mouth, to my horse. This is how they communicate to each other. The other horse, just wanted to visit my horse. There was one point in time, I told my Father about this horse. I said to him, this horse looks so beautiful. It was brown with white, like lightning streaks on its body. For myself, this horse looked like, a horse an Indian would ride. One day my Father, wanted to go to where the horse was, that I was talking about. We rode up to the house, and I waited in the car, and he went to the house, to talk to the people who owned the horse, to ask if it was for sale. I did not know he was going to ask them if the horse was for sale. I thought he just wanted to see it. When he walked to the house, and knocked on the door, the people came out. He asked them if the horse was for sale. They said, it was not. For this was fine for me. The horse was a special kind of horse, for it was very beautiful to look at, and the beauty was to behold. My Father and I, did behold the beauty of this horse. For to this very day, I love the beauty, that beholds horses, and their greatness of their strength. I have looked at them eye to eye, and talked with them, and felt a great communication. How they can be gentle animals, and they have a very unique understanding of their own.

I did some bareback riding, on a horse.

43

# Chapter Eleven

## Native American Indian beads, Myself, and Mother

Down the road for a little while from the Lake house. There was a town, but nothing much was there. Entering the town, then turning to the left, there was a store, it was a Native American Indian store. In the store, it had a long glass display case. In the glass display case, on the glass shelves, there were rows and rows of glass beads, of every color. They also sold Indian handmade items, that were made by the Indians in the area, and the people who owned the log cabin store, also made items that were sold in the store. The store was on an Indian reservation. In the same area they had an Indian pow wow. This is where they did traditional Native American Indian dances, that they did many, many years ago. They dressed in handmade outfits from their tribes. I once went to one, and the dancing was so greatly done. Next to the dancing, I walked over to where they had booths, and they were selling handmade Indian clothing, ponytail holders, bead jewelry, and all kinds of different furs, etc. For myself, seeing all these items, I knew I made some Indian jewelry, and ponytail holders for myself. Just like they were selling, I made the same kind all ready for myself, this was a good feeling.

At times when I would be at the lake house, I would go with my Mother in the car, past this little town, that had this Indian store, to a bigger town to buy food, and other things.

When we would go to the store, and when I was in the store, it was sometimes boring. But when my Mother said, pick out any kind of cereal I wanted for breakfast, this made shopping at this time better. For there were many times, my Mother and I would be in stores, and she asked me what I wanted. One place in time, I went to a big health food store, before we started shopping she said to me, I can have anything I wanted. At times we would start shopping, and when we were done my Mother said that she would pay for everything, and she happily did. For there were, some sayings my Mother said, to me many times. I would say to her, I love you, and she would say back to me, I love more. When we would be in some kind of conversation I would be saying no, then she would be saying yes. There was one time, I was with her, when she was in her house, she stood in the middle of the living room, and said to me, I am here because of you. I told her thank you, and then I was thinking, I knew that. I helped my Mother with my love, my true love from my heart.
We helped, and guided each other with health, and having the wisdom of it. We worked together and loved each other with everything that bonded us. For the bond we had as Mother and daughter was what it should be, and that love can be stronger than anything, when you have it as we did. I am her daughter, and I knew her longer than anyone ever could.
I am proud of my beautiful Mother, and I love her so greatly.
My Mother wore a lot of Native American Indian jewelry, she also wore clothes that had Native American Indian designs on them. She loved wearing these things, this made her proud, and she felt good and this made her all who she was.

Being very little, I would enjoy the iceman that came to my house. Every so often a little cute truck, would bring milk in glass bottles to the house. They would come in a holder, that was made of some kind of metal. The truck was very nice. I was outside in the front of the house; this was a hot day. The milkman came, up the driveway a little. I went up to the truck, to see him come out, before he brought the milk bottles to the house. I see that there were big blocks of ice, in back of the truck with the milk bottles. The day, was very hot. I was talking to the milkman, and telling him that it was so hot outside. He said, do you want a big piece of ice, because it is so hot. I said, with a big smile, and a great joy in myself yes. So the milkman went back in his truck, and got me a big piece of ice. Then after this, every time the milkman came to the house, to bring milk bottles for my Mother, I asked for ice or the milkman gave me a big piece of ice. With the ice I had, I chopped it up in pieces, and watched the pieces on the driveway melt in the hot sun. I would place a small piece of ice that I proudly chopped up, on my body to stay cool.
This is why I called him the iceman, ever since he gave me ice. He liked being called the iceman.
My Mother once said to me, any time I wanted to go out to dinner, on a Saturday night. Just call her and my Father, and we would go anyplace I wanted to go, and I did, and we went out almost every Saturday night, to the best restaurants in town, or in the area.

In kindergarten, I was asked to take a nap, I did not, I wanted to look over at my Grandmother's house, wanting not to be in the kindergarten room. I was wearing brand new clothes, as I always did. I would be looking over at my Grandmother's house, the teacher would say, Barbara take a nap, but I did not want too. I could see my

Grandmother's house across the street. I see her backyard, and the back of her house, and the beautiful flowers she grew. I did not want to be in Kindergarten, this was odd to me. When my Grandmother was right there, across the street. Sometimes my Mother wanted me to take naps, when I was very little, but I wanted to stay up to see anything that was happening in the house.

There was a time once, I was in Canada, in the impenetrable woods of Canada, next to a very clear lake. The lake looked wide, and the tall trees that looked perpetually, high to the sky. This was the most beautiful colors, of greens, of the trees, and the colors of blues in the sky, and the sky meeting the clouds. The clouds, danced as they moved around the sky.
In the dark of the night in the sky, there is stars that fill the sky. Stars in almost every part of the sky, as if a fairy threw a bucket of stars up to the sky, and they did not want to go. So they hang up there, waiting for a ride to go home. The stars, cover almost the dark of the sky, twinkling and sparkling as I look at them and hold them in my mind. The mountains, for me almost touched the sky, and the sky was touching the trees that were on the mountains, to form a blend of beauty, for only my eyes, and my heart to feel. There was a shore, and between the shore, there was grass, then the woods. I came out of the woods, and I walked on some grass. Then I looked at the water from the shore, before going into the water to swim. On the bottom, under the water at the shore, every so often I saw leaches. I wanted to swim in this clear, clean fresh water. So I watched where I stepped, then I walked between the leaches. I started to swim, I was swimming for a while. When I looked over at the shore. I saw a black bear, smelling the ground. I was thinking, oh my, Oh my, a black

47

bear. I thought if I wanted to come out of the lake, there is a black bear at the shore. I waited in the water, not knowing if bears can swim. I waited a little bit, and the black bear started walking slowly away some. Just for myself, to go to the shore, and when I was at the shore, I ran to the campsite. I do not camp, but this one time I did, and I had a black bear in my sight, and in my way.

# Chapter Twelve

## Mother, I Love you

When my Mother died, I was told three days after, lucky even that, because I stayed away from the people who gathered around her, and I could not go by her almost not at all, because the people were hard at me. My Mother would of never, ever wanted me to stay away from her, before she was dying, she always wanted me to help her, and she knew I could.

When I went once, to see my Mother in the hospital, I left a notebook in the room, that I wrote health foods, and who to contact that can help her, and other great things. I went to see my Mother a couple days later, and the book was gone, I know probably, why it was gone, but it should have stayed there. She would've wanted it. I knew my Mother, and she knew me, there was a bond, that people could not shake.

I did not go to her funeral, because I knew there were people who were just too hard, that I was over being anywhere by them. I have tried. I am a lot more sophisticated than they are. For myself, I would never ever do things, that they did to me. I am an example of a great human being. I know, after talking to other people that they would have never wanted anyone, to do what, people did to me. I tried to not have anything happen.

Where my Mother is buried, I went there by myself, to put real Lilies of the Valley flowers, on her grave. I got them from a home I lived at for a long time, the one my Father had built for me. Like my Grandmother, she had Lilies of the Valley flowers growing on the most sunniest part of her house. I even talked to my Mother, at her grave, about the people that did bad. My Father is buried, right next to her, so I was comforted by being next to both of them, when I talked. I cried, buckets full of tears, so much that there is a small pond around there, that my tears floated to the pond, where the ducks play. I was so hurt, and the ducks just were there to help me with some happiness. I know both of my parents heard me, and I know that they would have never ever let the people, who hurt me, let that happen at all.

My parents had love. But the other people did not. As I have said, the people never would have done this to me, if my parents were alive.

My parents had that much love, and the power they had was with the power of love, and working right with money, and their dreams they both made came true, with the perfectness of all the greatness, of themselves.

When my Mother died, I cried so much at different times. There was a time I cried for two weeks. I healed, but missing her and who she was to me, is all combined with the crying and health, that goes with that.

Power of love from a wonderful Mother, she gives to me every moment of every day, right at this moment now. I am her daughter, and we have a bond. My Mother is part of my life now, as she was when she was living. I was born from, my Mother and my Father, and I have what my parents were. I have this in myself, and my future.

When my Father died, it was two weeks later, I sang in front of a large group of people.

I cried when he died, for a long time, but I healed myself through this. I would hear my Father's good voice, how he talked to me, and that helped myself with the pain.

I also would hear how my Mother spoke, and that healed my pain. For me, their voice was very beautiful to hear. For, this matched who they both were as a human being.

Someone told me my Mother, was in the hospital at one place in time, not doing good. I went right to her, even when people told me not to go to her. For I did not listen to them, because I was better in life. I am part of my Mother's flesh, couldn't they get that in there, heart and mind. For there was no stopping me, to see my own Mother. When I saw her, she was not responding to anything, and she would not eat. I held her hand, and I got close to her. I told her I am here, and everything will be all right. I said this to her, over and over. I told her who I was, her daughter Barbara. I knew that she could hear me, I really knew. She knew how I live Holistic, and that we both have healed each other before. I went home, made food for her, she loved the way I made healthy, and healing food, I gave it to her, at her home all the time. After I made her the food, that I knew she should have, I brought it to her in the hospital, while she was laying there in bed. For my Mother in her whole life, it was about food, and the right ones to eat, she taught me this, and I taught her also. When my Mother and I, went in the grocery store we thought about the great ways of food, we did this together, this was her joy in life.
The next day I found out she ate my food, I knew she would, and she was coming out of what she was going through, at that moment. I brought to her, organic fruit, and other things. She then was sent home. I know I helped her as she came out of not responding, I guided the healing process. I know by myself, being at her side I could help her, and inside her she knew I could help her, this was something between my Mother and I.

I am saying this nice, there was someone just standing there, saying hi to me. I just passed the person, and I did not say, not a word to them. I just went right to my Mother, so I could help her as she would've wanted me too. I did help her as no one helped her, as I did. I was there for my Mother, and I helped her open her eyes, and talk.

There is a lot of negative about some people, of whoever I did write in my book about, but I did not want to write so much, I do not have that negative in my life, not anymore, I am gone from whatever people, that just wasted time hurting.

There was a time once, my Father would go out in the country, about 4 miles, from his home. To a farmhouse, that the people living there sold eggs. He would turn left, from the main road, onto a small country driveway to the farm. He then knocked on the old door. Someone would come and answer the door, then my Father went in. He went to buy eggs, but when he talked to the people selling them, he talked with them for a long time. So waiting for him in the car, it felt like a long time. My Mother loved fresh farm eggs, and the fact my Father, went to a farm to get them, made her happy. He also went to get the milk, on Saturday mornings, if there needed to be more milk, for the waffles. I made waffles from scratch at my parents' home, they loved them, and the waffles were very, **saporous, and delectable**.

My Mother and I went so many places together, if they were far like to Florida, or 10 miles away, or a block away. We traveled for hours, many times over night. I drove with my Mother, to a very large city, and we went to a jewelry store that is very well known throughout the world. I have been to this jewelry store, in many parts of the world. This was the first time my Mother was ever there. I know it was a magical place there as she stood in the store, and just

looked at so many beautiful jewelry pieces she never seen
before. This was a fairy land for her eyes. She told me, that
she had a good time. I wish she would've bought some
jewelry for herself.
My Mother as my Grandmother, did take care of their
home. She baked and cooked at times, I baked and
cooked better than she did, and she loved it. At times she
wanted to do other things.
One time my Mother was making a fruit bread, that had to
be kept still to rise, and set for a while, so it could rise
higher. Well then the bread, was being still and rising as it
should be, my Father came along and went to the bread,
and he wanted to try it. So he lifted the towel that was
placed on top of the rising bread. He then put his finger in
the bread to try it, and the bread started to slowly flatten.
My Mother came along, back into the kitchen, and she
looked at her bread, and said to my Father, what did you
do. She kind of, did not like that, but the story is a forever
one.
The fruit bread she made was like my Grandmothers, for
myself this was the greatest bread ever.
My Beautiful Mother, once gave me some money. The next
day I took some of the money she gave me, I went to the
store, and bought her some organic rose hand cream. I
bought her some health food that I knew she would of
loved, and healthy snacks also. I went to her house,
opened the door, and called her name. I went to her
kitchen table, I put everything on the table, and she stood
there, and looked at everything. I showed her the food, and
there was some rose hand cream. She picked up the rose
hand cream, and started putting it on her hands, then she
smelled the scent of the rose, and loved it. I told her I
bought these things, with some of the money that she gave

me. For she then, told me the money was for me. This was one of the ways, she was to me, and I was to her back. With a big Breath, as I breathe, as I am writing this, and I am about to cry, and my tears are ready to come down my cheeks, I will let them come.
There are deep feelings of missing a person that I totally and unconditionally love, in my heart, and now.
For myself to say this, this was the last time I seen my Mother in person, for I never seen her again.
But I did call her on the phone at times, before she died. I called her, and I sang to her, and she sang with me, on the phone, then she told me, I am the singer, and I was. At this point, I did not, hear her voice anymore, or get to be with her.
I feel a touch on top of my head, as I write this. This is my Mother, saying it is all right.
I love her, and she loved me, as she would say, I love you more, Barbara.
I really miss my Mother, and she misses me.
This is moving for my heart, at this point. This is a connection with my heart beat.


Gingerbread House
Starting with the roof made of gingerbread, and the four sides made out of Gingerbread.
Gingerbread House is about five in a half feet tall, and five feet wide.
There is white buttercream frosting on top of the roof. Then all the outsides of the Gingerbread House, is buttercream frosting. There is a window on each side, and a door in front of it. Gumdrops, are put on all over, and they are being held on by the buttercream frosting. Ribbon candy, in its ribbon shape, with all different colors, delicately set on, in perfect places.

When I was very young, I went with my Mother to the little bakery, five blocks from my Grandmother's house. My Mother would do special orders, buns or other bakery. I went with her to pick them up.

Each time I opened the bakery door, or my Mother did, I first can smell the wonderful bakery. The very first sighting I can see, is the Gingerbread House. This is around Christmas time. My first sighting of the most Beautiful House in the world is the Gingerbread House. As the Bakery door opens, I go over to the Gingerbread House. I stand here for a while, looking at all the candy, that is put on top of the buttercream frosting. The Gingerbread House is designed so **Magical**, so **Dreamy**, and there is a **Fairy Tale** existence, living in it and being happy. A House with candy on it, that can be eaten, and to **Dream**.

This is a very special moment, about this Gingerbread house, who built the House, who lives in the House.

This Gingerbread House is in the middle of a small bakery, where my Mother picked up her special orders, and came in for some bakery, time to time. I was the Happiest child in the world, to come with my Mother. To see the biggest **Gingerbread House** with Buttercream Frosting for paint, and candy for Decorations.

The whole Gingerbread House is sprinkled with powdered sugar, and this looks as if it snowed early this morning.

The smell of this house, does have a smell of wake up in the morning, or anytime.

This Gingerbread house is a happy house, and it is Beautiful.

# Chapter Thirteen

## My Singing, and the Greatest Gentleman to me

After my Father died, I started painting more, on the table, there was the paper, or canvas to paint on, and the brushes. When I was going to start painting I felt sadness, but I picked the brush up, and I got paint, and started painting. The paintings I did were ostentatious, and beautifully done. It was like I lit right up, with my art. When my Father, was dying, I was the only one he knew that was out in the room, wanting to see him, and help him. After he knew, I was there, he died a few days later. For myself, this was the most hardest thing, on myself, knowing he died. Right now, I am very emotional right at this moment, writing these few sentences. I am so like him, there is a very strong, sense of forever love I have for the most wonderful gentleman in the world my great Father. I miss him, every moment, but the most wonderful thing is I am like he was, and now to me. I live, he lives in my heart, and in my life, I stand up for him, and he is proud of me, and I am proud of my Father, I am proud of myself.
My Father could have lived more, if people could have loved him more, and showed love to him, as he loved the people that should've loved him.
For my Father, was the only one I ever knew who had a heart of Gold. He was a man that did everything.

When I was very young, I was there when my Father polished his shoes, because he was a salesman, before he was the President of his own Company.
When I first learned to sew, the thing I made was a tie for him. When I was very young he gave me horseback rides to bed.
There will never be enough to say about this man my Father, or how I feel for him in love.

Moment in time, I was at my Mother's house, doing something. The phone rang, I picked up the phone, someone told me my Father fainted at his Company. I told the person thank you for telling me. My Mother was gone for some length of time. I stopped what I was doing. Got in my car, and went over to him. When I got there, they were putting him in an ambulance. While they were doing this, they asked me if I wanted to go with him, to be with him. They thought that I was his wife. This is twice someone thought I was his wife; I think this is so cute. I said no, I did not want to go into the ambulance, when they were putting him in there, because I wanted them to help him right away. To this very day, I would have gone with my Father, I could have helped him in the ambulance, and be there, right next to him. For to see him, laying that way was something I was not wanting to see him do, because I wanted to help him.
For he was a towering strength, when I was a child, and when I got older. He was a real man, a very rare person, and my Father had a heart full of love, and compassion. What I did, I went with my car, and followed my Father to the hospital. I was shaking in the car, when I was following my Father. I just wanted to know how he was doing. When I got to the hospital I sat and waited, to know something. I asked someone to tell my Father, I was there, and I

wanted to see him. They asked him, and they came back
to tell me, he did not want to see anyone right now,
because he was throwing up. Then time passed, and I see
him when they wheeled him passed me to take him to
surgery.
Later in the days, I seen him with a tube in his head. When
I talked with him, I held his hand, and I told him who I was,
and the machine next to him, was making noise. I know
this noise was the fact that my Father could hear me, and
that inside of him, he wanted to respond. I knew he could
hear me, and he could feel. I was telling him, over and over
that I loved him, I loved him so much. For all the while I
was telling him, I loved him very much, I was holding his
arm.
For this was the last time I ever saw him.
About three or four days later, I stood on stage, and sang
at his funeral. I sang a song he liked. Someone asked me
how I could sing, at that moment in time, I just did.
If I could bring back, both of my Parents I would. I did not
want him to die, for myself he was a man that was super
great, and I know people, put pressures on him and he
should have not listened to them.
For to this very day, I did not listen to those people, and I
never will, I am away from them now, and my parents
should've been also. This is a world away, and a world
difference. I love this. But my parents are in me, and in my
life, they are safe this way, with me.
The thing about, me singing at my Father's funeral,
someone told me not to sing.
I was not going to listen, I sang, and everyone watched.
I was not crying at the time, because he was so much,
alive in my life, and he was alive in life, that I see.
Later I cried, and it was very hard.

Today, I imagine, and I create, and I am smart, with the gifts my parents gave me.

One night I was driving by my Father's company. I see him sitting next to the window working on something. He looked very pale, and white. He looked stressed. The next day it was when, the phone rang, and it was about that he fainted at his company. He worked hard, with compassion to have his own company, and he was proud that his parents both knew, what he did, and that he had his own company.
For the love he had could circle the world.
He said, to me even before he died. That he would pay for all my schooling, and where I wanted to go. I thought about this, and I wanted this. I was going to tell him, that he could pay for my schooling, that very night, I seen him at his office sitting there working hard. He was pale and stressed that one night and I was going to tell him about school, days later, after I seen him that night. This was going to be good news for him, and myself. At this point in time, I did not want to stress him, for it was evening, and he was working at night, when he did not have too.
My Father was so good and gentle, he loved everything he did in his life.
For myself years later, I went to a Great University for about 4 years, for my singing, with my voice. This was as if, a touch doing, because of talking with my Father, as he talked about school to me. I was singing, before I went to the University, and sang after, I then turned professional.
It was one evening; I was driving through a small town. Then I came to a swamp, that I had to pass over, as I was driving. The moon was very enchanting, and the trees in the swamp were thick, and dense, the colors were beautiful. I finished coming out of the swamp, to come to

open fields, and woods rich with their colors. The sun was going down, more at this point, but still it was just very enchanting with the clear fresh air, and myself. I came to the town; I was driving too. I went into the building, and before I started to sing, I told the people that my Father passed away 2 weeks ago. I said he is giving to me, the strength to sing. There was a large group of people. This all went well. I was done singing, and then I was driving passed the woods, and through the enchanting swamp. There was the light of the moon, shining in my direction, letting me know, this is all beautiful, and good.

My singing Professor, loved salsa, and loved making it homemade. I once was singing next to her baby grand piano, while she played the music. When we were done, she asked me a question, would I take her to a friend's house, they lived next to a big park. They had a garden in their backyard, filled with tomatoes. I told her I would take her. So I took her, when we got there we both went in the backyard, to the garden, and picked a lot of tomatoes, they were big and red. While we were picking the tomatoes, she said to me I can have some tomatoes, so I picked more, and later when we were done picking tomatoes, I ate them with my heart's content. The tomatoes, were big and juicy, and healthy. My Professor made salsa from the tomatoes, one time I was singing to her, and she gave me some homemade salsa, she made, it was so fresh, and good. After she made her salsa, she would put it on her table in rows to cool. The sun rays, through her windows, would shine on the jars of salsa, making them even better looking, and tasting.

I drove to Nashville, Tennessee for a while, to show record labels my singing. I went there two different times to

Nashville, Tennessee for my singing. When I was in Nashville, I talked with a wife of a person who is a Country superstar, singer. The wife was a Southern Lady, and she was very nice to talk too. She said to me, she will see me on the television. For me that was nice for her to say. On the drive to Nashville, Tennessee on the main road to the city. I see the bus of the Country music superstar, who is married to the wife, that I talked with. When I drove in Nashville, I came to a stop, on a corner that I was going to make a turn. When I stopped, I turned my head, and right there standing proud, and beautiful was the Ryman Auditorium. I did not know where it was, but it just came to me, and I came to it. This was a showing of protecting me, for I did not know the city at all. But I know my singing. People of greatness, sing and perform at the Ryman Auditorium, who are the best Country music singers in the world.

Music is something my Mother loved. I sang, and wrote songs, to sing to her, a lot of times I would call her, wherever she would be, and I would sing to her on the phone. Sometimes she would, sing with me, she unconditionally loved all of this.

# Chapter Fourteen

## I am part, Native American Indian, and Prussian

I am part Native American Indian. I am part Native American Indian from my Grandfather, on my Mother's side of the family. The kind of Indian is Brotherton Indian. It is also, named Brothertown Indian. I was told they settled in Stockbridge, Wisc. U.S.A. I was told this story. But there is more to the story.
The Brothertown Indians created a settlement called, Eeyamquittoowauconnuck it was later named, the town Brothertown, the Native American Indian tribe, of my Grandfather's people, came from the southern New York area. They came in boats, on the Great Lakes, then they went to Lake Winnebago in Wisconsin. My Mother told me about my Grandfather Being Native American Indian. I am very proud, and distinguished of all this. Brothertown Indian, speak Mohegan language. I can speak some Mohegan, and I can write some Mohegan.

Prussian from Prussia,

On my Father's side of the family, my Great Grandfather, and my Great Grandmother, came from Prussia, Europe, then they went to America. When my Great Grandfather,

and my Great Grandmother, had to flee, and knew that
they needed to leave Prussia their homeland, they needed
to leave very fast. They thought about what they were
going to pack, and they put it on a cart with a horse pulling
it. My Great Grandfather, and my Great Grandmother had
to leave very fast. The hooves on the horse were wearing
down, because the horse was running so fast to get out of
there. This was a story that was told to me. For to this day,
I am proud of my Great Grandfather, and my Great
Grandmother, and I am like them in my life.
I know how it feels, to leave something very fast, for when
this happened to me, my Great Grandparents were with
me every minute of it. I have a strong connection to them. I
have lived there for a length of time, very close to where
my Great Grandfather, and my Great Grandmother was
born, I felt very much at home where they started their life
in Prussia. I was happy there, to have that connection, and
feelings, that is a part of my life to this very day. I am proud
of my last name and I am proud, that I carry this with me
wherever I go.
From my Great Grandparents, to my Grandfather, to my
Father, they have given to me the Love, and total strength
in myself.
My Great Grandfather was born in Saatzig, Prussia,
Europe. My Great Grandmother was born in Klein Raddow,
Prussia, Europe. Born in the Pomeranian area, Prussia.
My Great Grandfather's Mother would spin the wool, and
his Father did the knitting. My Great Grandmother's
parents had a farm, and raised sheep. My Great
Grandmother learned to be a seamstress, and became a
maid for wealthy people. They both came to America, and
lived in a small log cabin on a road that is called for their
last name. My Father's Grandfather at one time in his life,
worked at a sawmill in a very small town. About every 3

months he would walk home to the log cabin home. My
Great Grandfather wanted my Great Grandmother to
move, to where he was working.
But my Great Grandmother would say no, because she did
not speak English, and she was afraid people in the town
would ridicule her.
With my Great Grandfather's earnings at the sawmill, he
then purchased land, and became a full time farmer, also
raising sheep. My Great Grandfather also taught my Great
Grandmother to knit.
I was told this story.
Prussia, is a mix from lands Finland, or Sweden, or Russia,
or Norway. They are proud of being Prussian, from
Prussia. This meant everything to them.
This is another story told to me.
My Great Grandfather had beautiful clear blue eyes. My
Great Grandfather was a thin man, my Grandfather was a
thin man, my Father was a thin man, I am a thin woman,
this is pasted down.
My Father was deeply proud of where he came from, and
of his Grandparents, where they came from, and what they
had. Before my Father died, he was going to go to Europe.
I went to Europe, for both myself, and my Father. I am
proud, I am part Prussian.

For there is deep sorrow that pains so bad, and there is
deep love that has overflowing amount of joy, and forever
happiness that is a constant. I had them both at the same
time. But the most, **rhythmical**, and **ostentatious** of these
is a constant amount of deep love of forever, happiness of
perfect happiness.
My Father sang a song, that he was taught from his
Grandparents.
I can speak some Prussian, and I am learning more.

Prussia was a Country; Prussia was right next to the Baltic
Sea. Prussia had a King with a Crown, and there is a
castle. There was and is a language of Prussian, it was
and it still is written down, and spoken, it can be called old
Prussian, or Prussian.
The country was a beautiful country, my Great
Grandparents must of had beautiful times there, before
they were forced to leave. Maybe Prussia, can be called
old Prussia, but it is just Prussia to me.

# Chapter Fifteen

## Farm, and Lake House, both deep in my Heart

This starts from the city, driving to a little diner in a very small town. The diner was all white, with a covered porch in the front. This was not just little it was old. I got fish, and French fries with catsup, they put all the food in a small basket to eat out of it. Then back into the car, passed, the stop and go lights, to an ice cream shop that sold a lot of different kinds of ice cream. I always got two scoops of blue moon, flavored ice cream. The ice cream tasted so delicious. Then back in the car to go farther down the road. On the right side of the road, there is a small red cabin, in front of the cabin there is a tall wooden pole, maybe 13 feet high. On top of the pole is a mailbox, colored red with white paint saying the words air mail. I think, how can the mail person get up there, or does birds fly up there to mail the letters. Riding in the car, coming close to the bait shop to buy some bait, for fishing, at the house on the lake, got the bait and came out of the shop, then I got in the car. Then after the bait shop, through the woods lots of woods, and on the small roads to the lake house.
I was the first one in the family to go water skiing. A friend asked me to go water skiing, and she was going to teach me, so the offer was good, and I have watered skied ever since.

I realize to this very day that I can connect to the woods,
because of the clear air from the trees, and other things
that make up the woods, that they purely have.
I connect to the woods, because at a young age I lived
next to them, for a long part of my life. I lived in the city, so
I am a city person and a country-woods person.

My Father grew up on a farm. When I was very young I
would go with my Parents, to were my Grandparents lived
on the farm, where my Father grew up. My Father only
went to 8th grade in his education. This is how it was way
back in time for some people. My Father walked through
open fields and some woods from his home on the farm to
a small one room school building to where he went to
school. I see the land where the school was. He wanted to
have more education as my Mother, has said to me. But he
made a grand business with his company, and his life was
amazing.
Going to the farm, was something very very special in my
mind, and forever it stays.

In the barn just a little walk from the house. I was very little,
and I wanted to see the cows. People were talking about
the cows in the house all the time. So I went outside, and I
walked to the barn. The door was opened a little, and I
opened it more so I could go in. The barn smelled, like
fresh cow smell. I used to like that smell, but it is just ok
now. I recall, there was a lot of cows, making their noises. I
went in, I just stood there, at one end of the barn. I knew if
I could go behind the cows, pass behind them while they
were eating. I could run to the other side of the barn, and
pass them, for me this would be great. So I ran passed the
cows, as fast as my little legs could go. I was so very
young at this point of time. I made it to the other end of the

barn, and I passed the cows, and I thought I was the greatest, I did this all myself. The cows being inside the barn, this was fun for me.

When I was there at my Father's home, where he grew up on the farm, I was very young. At the farmhouse there were woman in the kitchen cooking, baking, laughing, and talking as they baked and cooked. I would be in the living room, and there were people playing the piano, and singing and talking. I was so little at this time, and knowing all of this, for myself it has a white, and yellow look of seeing it, every time this is recalled in myself. This has a great power to it, and it is something I knew, and I had for real in my life, and forever. I love this.

My Father sometimes went over to milk the neighbor's cows.

I also know in the farmhouse there was a large stone staircase leading up to the upstairs. For myself being so very little, and as I was standing at the bottom of the staircase, looking up, it was high, very high up, and very grand of a staircase to me, I thought what is up there, it must be so very grand.

To this very day, I know how to get to the farmhouse from wherever I am, I know it that well.

My Great Grandfather that started the land, and the homestead. He would walk from his home, and it took him days to walk, to where he worked, and he would stay there awhile, then walk home. This is something that I do in my life, I walk so much. Doing what he did was more work of the doing, then just thinking about it.

My Grandmother on my Mother's side. She lived for her home, and working in the kitchen. She made for me, the best food in the world. Her pies, were so delicious. She made everything always homemade. She walked to the grocery store, and it was about four blocks from her home. My Mother would drive my Grandmother to a different grocery store every Thursday, and she would take her for lunch, they all loved it.

What I did when I was very young, I put a chair in front of the oven, and watched the food my Grandmother made, if she was cooking or baking. I still at times like to watch food in the oven, when it is baking or cooking and I am making it.

I played kicked the can at the lake house, and in the city. This is a game played in the evening. There is a can, and someone stands by the can, then other people just go to different places and hide. Then after that, the first one who kicks the can without being seen, wins the game.

This was real fun.

This book is about a life I had, I could say, Fairy Tale life. There were very hard moments that I never needed, or wanted. But the life was Fairy Tale, with Fairies opening my eyes up, lifting me out of ugliness, and keeping me in the air high above everything else. Only until it was safe, and comfortable, and only when it was the very best, and the most beautiful, would the fairies bring me back down, to the place I really needed to be.

# Chapter Sixteen

## Diamonds, Cowboys, and Leather laced boots

I walked to school when I was young, if my Mother did not drive me to school. For, when I walked to school it was about 1 in a half mile to school. This was very creative for me. When the snow was melting, there would be crystals forming on the snow, this looked like to me, jewels sparkling on the snow. I felt as if I just seen something more beautiful, than I could ever tell anyone. For this was for myself, in my heart. For to this day, when there is snow on the ground, and the sun shines down upon it, there is sparkles, just as real as diamonds, that sparkle in the right light. For a diamond shines so unique, and they are from under the ground. For they both have the same sparkle of sunlight, on the white snow, and on the diamonds, when the sun shines on them. For this is the beauty to behold in the eyes. It was a long time, until I seen a real diamond. That I knew the sparkle on the snow, that I see when I was very young, matched the sparkle of the diamond I seen.

My Mother was always so proud that she walked, most places she went to, when she was young, I walked so many places, when I was young. To say right now, one of my happiest things to do is walk as many places my feet are going to walk. In the woods is the greatest.
When I sailed on the lake, the wind would blow the sail, and the wind was so refreshing, going on my face. I loved the wind, it could be warm at times, or it could be cool. The

smell of air from the woods blowing in the wind, all felt
great and this guided myself as I sailed on the water.
My Father drove from the top of a state, down to almost
the bottom, he like to drive. He drove through one state,
then through another state, then down to the last state. He
drove his semi-truck that he had, to pick up antique
tractors. Tractors that he bought, and had his mechanic fix
them, so he could use them, for when he went to tractor
pulls. For there was a time I went with him to buy, and pick
up an antique tractor. This was the time he drove his semi-
truck through, three different states. He was driving for a
while, and I see a rest stop. I said to him, this is telling you
to rest. He just kept on going.
After a while he did stop, and he took a nap.
We got to the place where he was going to buy the tractor,
it was outside of an Indian Reservation. The people
greeted us kindly. They asked us to have lunch, with them
and we did. The food was all homemade, even the pickles
were in their own jar. The food was so good, and we were
very hungry.
They loaded the antique tractor, onto the semi-truck. We
said thank you for the food, then we left. This was a long
ride back. As my Father was driving his semi-truck, I would
see cattle in the hills, the cattle were coming down, to
cross the road in front of us. At one point, I seen some
cowboys with their hats, chaps, boots, and their cowboy
coats. On their cowboy boots, down in the back by the
heel, on the outside of the boots, they wore spurs. The
cowboys were working the spurs to move the horse, they
were riding on, so the cattle would be guided. The
cowboys were in great shape, and they had good looking
faces. They were heading cattle across the road, right in
front of us. When I see the cowboys, riding on their horses
and the cows were in front, and in the back, and on the

sides of the cowboys, there was dust moving all around
them, all over the place. My Father had to slow down a lot,
and he came to a complete stop, on the road, right next to
the cows, and the cowboys. After the cows, and cowboys
passed, I wanted my Father to honk his horn in the semi-
truck, and he did. I waved to the cowboys, and they waved
back to me. I was so happy to be there, and I am part
Indian, this was all great. They were real cowboys, doing
what real cowboys do, it is great being a cowboy.

Someone asked me to ride a Tennessee walker type of
horse. I have never ridden one before. This horse is very
high in height, higher than other horses. I rode it, and the
person who wanted me to ride it, said to me, not just
anyone can ride a Tennessee walker horse, they are very
high off the ground for just anyone to ride. But I rode it
gently, and I walked the horse beautifully, and wonderfully.
I did it. For myself, I have ridden a lot of horses.
Sometimes with horses, I feel as the horse whispers knows
the horse, in that different way, I can also connect to them.
My Father and I were both around horses a lot.
What my Father was, is a man who meant the world to me.
I deeply, and forever, and in perpetuum, love my great
Father. I feel this in my heart right now. I am glad, and
proud, I am like him, and there was no other man as him,
and there never will be, he was and is one of a kind.

One night, I was sleeping at my parents' home, I happened
to be sitting on the floor that evening, my Father came and
sat down next to me, he asked me to go on a sales trip
with him for about three days. I said yes. This was a
dreamy time. We took a plane to the state of Montana, and
to different towns, and two other states also. At one point, I
sat next to my Father, and he said to me, I should wear

tailored clothes. I did not say anything. When he said this to me, I was wearing a leather fringed coat, that had fringe on the arms, and fringe on the bottom of the brown leather coat. I was also wearing boots, and they were brown leather, that came high to my knees, and they laced in the front, starting at my knee, and all the way down to my feet. I looked the part, cowgirl, and part Indian, and the fact is I am part Indian, so I felt the part.

It was cute, one moment in time, when my Father and I, were on this trip, we were at the airport waiting for a plane in the Denver, Colorado airport. There was a Lady, that came over to us, and asked if we were married. I smiled a great big smile, and I said no, then I looked at my Father. For to this day, I always wear tailored clothes, because I love to, and I always dress great, this is because of my Father, once telling me to wear tailored clothes, on the plane flying over glaciers, and lakes, and mountains, high above the Rocky Mountains. Flying with my Father, above the beautiful white wild mountain goats, that walk on the mountains, and take shelter on them, and the other wild animals that live down there, with the beautiful Spruce trees, and Birch trees, and other trees.

How my Mother, went to the stores with me to pick out clothes, and how she dressed me when I was very very young, and how I dress myself now, is a perfect delight. For my Father saying this about tailored clothes to me, this is what I want.

From watching my wonderful Father, shine his shoes with joy, when I was very young, and thinking that this was super great. To being his daughter, and being happy I had a Father, that was a man, that I knew, and I truly know that I loved, he is my Father and a human being that is part of myself, and my Mother's love.

For my Parents, Loved each other.

They gave me, a part of a human being, that no one could
have ever done.
I Thank them both, and I am glad, and happy with this.

# Chapter Seventeen

## His Majesty the King and Her Majesty the Queen, with a Royal Crown

Standing outside of the palace, on a beautiful clear day. A man dressed with a hat, that was long in the front, that came to some kind of point, at the end. With an old fashion outfit on, that came right out of a story book. The outfit was very official, and very important in protecting the Palace, and His Majesty the King, and Her Majesty the Queen in their home. He came up to me, and asked me if I wanted to go to the inner courtyard of the Palace, to see as His Majesty the King, and Her Majesty the Queen were welcoming a very special, and important guest. Who was a President of their own Country. I quickly said yes, and he said to follow him. I was so elated; this is my thing in life. I did follow him as he guided me, as I walked on rocks, that were hundreds of years old, the rocks to me were beautiful rocks. I was walking behind him, and at that very moment I felt very much like a princess, doing duties as a princess would be doing. Walking over the rocks, I went to the Palace door. There before me was a humongous wooden door. This was an ostentatious design of a door, and the door handles were beautifully made, they looked as if an old fashioned blacksmith, hundreds of years ago, made them, I think they did.

I myself standing here, looking at this door, ready to go in and see His Majesty the King, and Her Majesty the Queen, and for me to be in their presence.

The door opens, I walk proudly through, to the inner
courtyard of the Palace. Here I am, and I was asked to be
here. I was appointed to stay at a certain place, and I did.
The Palace was ostentatious, and Breathtakingly,
Beautiful. For myself this is, if I was in my home.
One side of the courtyard, there were horses standing at
attention, the horses were beautiful brown, and beautiful
white, they were all beautiful. Next to the horses is a band
playing music. The horses just stood, at great attention,
they looked royal just waiting for His Majesty the King, and
Her Majesty the Queen to make their presence.
Then on the other side of the inner courtyard, people were
waiting for the very important person, the President coming
to visit, from the invitation by His Majesty the King, and Her
Majesty the Queen. I waited, then I turned around, as I am
standing by the opening of the wooden door. I looked out
of the big door, and seen the open carriage, with His
Majesty the King, and the President, sitting in the beautiful
open carriage with horses pulling it, coming to the Palace.
The horses were, making a gallop, as they were moving.
There was footman on the open carriage, and a coachman
on the open carriage, he was driving the horses, the
footman and the coachman, were all dressed, in
appropriate uniforms, as in a story book.
This way of life, is all for today as it was hundreds of years
ago.
For His Majesty the King, and Her Majesty the Queen's
way of life, and the life of their country. This is real, and
story book, for real.
I watched as the horses pulling the open carriage, with His
Majesty the King, and the President were in the open
carriage. They went passed, as they were going to, the
other part of the Palace, to come in where I was waiting.
The horses came in, pulling the open carriage with His

Majesty the King, and the President. The horses stopped. The two men stepped down, and out of the open carriage. His Majesty the King walked to where the band was playing. Then the President walked, to His Majesty the King and they greeted each other warmly.

With all this going on, Her Majesty the Queen was standing, in one part of the courtyard watching as the President came to greet His Majesty the King. Her Majesty the Queen was dressed grandiloquent; her dress was blowing in the wind. Her Majesty the Queen was standing there with love for His Majesty the King, and the love of her country. I could see that Her Majesty the Queen was beautiful in the inside, and all of who she is on the outside. Her Majesty the Queen watched, and had an exquisite smile on her face.

His Majesty the King, and the President, came over to Her Majesty the Queen, and all three of them went over to greet the important people who were watching them. When they were done, His Majesty the King, and the President, and Her Majesty the Queen were smiling as they walked into the Palace.

That very night there was a Grand dinner, as the King, and the Queen honored their guest, to the finest food from the King, and Queen. They all dined on the best food that the royal chiefs prepared, according to the wishes of the King, and Queen. This went on, with the beautiful moonlight outside, shining ever so brightly, and the twinkling of the stars in the sky, as the stars watched from above, smiling with joy.

The King, and the Queen of their country, can be proud of their country, and all the Breathtaking beauty of the land. For this happened, and I was like a princess for a time. For dreams come true.

When the horses and the open carriage, left out from the
inner courtyard. The horses pulling the open carriage,
came right next to me, and I was looking right at the eyes
of a horse. I was so close to the horses, that I could have
touched one of the horses. While the horses and the open
carriage were passing next to me, I see this, all so close to
me, everything is so very grand and beautiful, and the
coachman were controlling the reins of the horses. The
open carriage had a gold painted crown on the side of the
open carriage, and the open carriage was brown.
The coachman and the other people working with the open
carriages have unique, and special clothing they wear,
only when they are working with the horses, and the
carriages for the King, and Queen, and the Royal Family,
of the land. The outfits look like, as in storybooks. They are
very real now.
This is a moment in time, in a wonderful piece of time.
For this is a wonderful land, and a bright ray of beautiful
sunshine.

# Chapter Eighteen

## The Smell of the, Lily of the Valley Flower

I love the smell of the Lily of the Valley flower, they are very fresh, as the morning dew smells, in the Springtime. The Lily of the Valley flower is a very special flower.

My Mother loved to make a smile on people's faces. Many times I seen my Mother smile at people as they passed by her, this could be at any place. I see the people smile back at her. She said to me, make fun out of it, whatever it maybe. This is wise of her, and true.

For there was a special time and place, I waved to Her Majesty the Queen in an open carriage, and I said her name, because she is a special Queen. As I waved, she seen me, and then she turned her head, and started to talk to His Majesty the King who was riding in the same open carriage, sitting right next to her. I think at that moment I was maybe talked about, when the King, and the Queen were talking. For the Queen, had the same name as my Mother.

I was doing too much work at one period of time. My Mother heard about it, and she bought me a pink feather Christmas tree, to put a smile on my face.
One time, My Mother asked me when I was very young, to feed my little sister her baby food. I did not know how to feed her the baby food, so I ate it. The flavor was some kind of fruit, and I thought it was really good.

Every Sunday morning my Father got in his car, when we were in the city. He went to the corner of a street, where someone was selling the Sunday morning newspaper. This was a part of his life that was fun for him.

My Father loved, being in the woods and he went to the woods, as much as he could, for this was a great love of his, and this is a great love of mine too. He grew up in the country, and his heart was always there.

Both of my parents, liked the fact that I sang.

My Father had someone build me a house, then he gave it to me. I was so overjoyed, and loved both of my parents, even so much more. I painted part of the garage door, I painted the door going into the house. I also painted under the eaves troughs around the house. For myself, to paint under the eaves troughs, my Father drove a machine, like a tractor, with a front scoop on it and I stood in it, and then I could paint. When I got done painting a section, my Father would move the machine, over to the other parts to be painted. We got the painting finished, and both of us were proud to have it done.

I had a big garden with herbs, and vegetables and lots of different flowers, the flowers were growing all different places around the house. This made the outside, smell very good, and very beautiful. There were Blue Spruce trees in a row, in the back of the house. My Father, had them planted for me, because I love Blue Spruce trees, they smell wonderful, and they are grand to look at. The Blue Spruce trees, have soft blue color needles, and on their branches, they can be compared with the blues of the sky, when the sky is the same color. The sky changes colors of blue.

Blue Spruce trees have pine cones, that grow on them. I love this.

In front of the house, that was built for me, there were Lily
of the Valley flowers outside, in the corner of the house.
Every year there would be more Lily of the Valley flowers,
as they multiplied in numbers.
The smell of the Lily of the Valley flowers, is for myself
spring time, and fresh and divine.
Another flower that is spring time, is the Iris flower, I go to
the plant, I take two petals, I move them apart gently, and
then I smell the middle of the flower between the petals,
and then there is spring.
My Grandmother, had Lily of the Valley flowers growing on
the side of her house. She absolutely loved flowers, she
was working in her garden all the time. She also had
flowers growing next to her kitchen window. She had glass
shelving, that her plants would sit on, so they could
capture the sunshine rays, to have them grow. The sun
came in strong, in the windows that faced the west. Her
plants grew beautiful to behold. She was a Lady to be
remembered, and that she had all the Love you think you
need. She was very comforting. She loved to smile, my
Mother did also. My Grandmother was content with her life,
for myself that was amazing to me. I miss her always, and
forever, she is in every part of myself, and I am very much
like my Grandmother on my Mother's side. My
Grandmother and I were very close, we still are as she is in
my heart, and mind now.

When I shopped with my Mother for clothes, she always
wanted me to try them on and model them, so she could
see how they looked on me. She would say, could you
model the clothes now, when I found something I liked.
She loved seeing me in new clothes all the time. This
brings it back, to when I was very young, and my Father

said to my Mother, buy some new clothes for her, or he would say buy her some new shoes.

The shoe store, one of them at that time, had old wooden floors, old lights and was an old building, but they sold new shoes, in those times, they were beautiful shoes, I loved them. I had the best shoes, then anyone who was ever next to me. I still recall sitting on the old wood chair, having my Mother sitting next to me, watching me trying on new pairs of shoes, to find out which one would fit right, so I could have them, this was a world to live in, and this was mine.

I recall the post office that was, big and grand, and beautiful. For the stairs to walk up to the grand building, the post office, were beautiful and wonderful, and there were enough stairs to walk up. When I got up to the building, I opened the large ornately made wooden doors, and as I went inside, I looked down at the marble floors. For to this very day, I recall this grand place, I was very young when I first went here. The stairs were as if I was walking up to a Palace, or a Castle. This old post office is not there anymore. But I knew it was there, and I have seen it.

When I was young, and I thought if I was going to marry. I would come out of the church wearing a white satin dress, made of French material, the veil would be all lace. I would wear a red velvet cape, with a white fur hood, and I would have a white fur muff, to keep my hands warm, because it would be snowing beautifully outside. Then I would step up, into the open carriage, and I would have magnificent looking white horses, pulling me away from there.

When I was young, I was always dressed great, better than anyone next to me. I went into the stores, from big department stores to Boutiques, and I got anything I wanted to wear. If I had all the clothes I ever had, I would have about three Boutiques full of my clothes.

There was a time when I was young, Doctors were making house calls all the time. This was a normal happening. They tried to do healthy ways first to heal. My Mother did, a lot of what they said.

# Chapter Nineteen

## Empress of Austria, Castle

Very high on the side of a mountain, high where the air is perfectly clear. High up here on this mountain I woke up, in the morning. I look out of the window, at the perfectly clear air, and I see the lake that is clean, and fresh. I can see that the water is clear, and clean, because the water came from the Magnificent mountain, where I woke up at. The trees are so tall, if I open the windows, I could touch them. For these trees are different than any trees I have seen. The trees are living in the mountain air, and drinking the mountain water. They live on the mountain, that takes care of them, as they take care of themselves. I walked down, the old wooden ornately carved staircase, to go to breakfast. As I walk, there is a grand feeling I feel as I walk on each step. I can see out some windows, how just breathtaking it is outside, I just want to touch it, hold it in my hands, and keep it forever lasting. This is kept in my heart, and I have it kept in my deepest part of myself, and my mind works with it.

I come to the breakfast room, there is Black tea, Chamomile tea, Green tea, Rosehip with fresh Alpine mountain herb tea. There are croissants, and fresh country mountain brown bread with sunflower seeds on the outside of the bread. This bread is to be cut, slice by slice. There are eggs from the farmer down the mountain road. There is fresh made juices. There is Hot Chocolate. I ate breakfast, the one thing I always have is Hot Chocolate. Their Hot Chocolate, is so thick it is getting to be pudding, but not pudding. The Chocolate, is Dark Chocolate the way I love it.

I went outside, and walked over to the garden that is right next to the Castle. The garden has raspberries plants, and they are brightly red raspberries that are ready to be picked. I picked some with my hands, then I ate them right away. The difference of picking them with my hands, is the berries are growing in the perfect mountain air, and having the mountain rain water, sprinkled ever so gently on the plants. The taste is sheer delight for me. For this has me feel great. There are other things growing in the garden. I heard the birds, singing a musical orchestra, so the whole woods can hear, I can hear them beautifully. I see the squirrels, climbing on the tall tree trunks, and hopping to the tree branches, smiling as they do. I walked for just a little bit more. There is an orchard with apples that are ready to be picked, some are pink, and some are red, I picked a beautiful pink one. Later I washed it, and ate the apple, this was one of the best apples I have had.

From the orchard I look over, and next to it is a small pond, and there is brightly yellow somewhat, thin and tall swamp Iris flowers, growing on the edge of the pond. There is an enchanting, exquisite feeling, when I am standing here at this pond. I hear frogs, making their wonderful noises. The sun is shining on the pond differently than anywhere else, there is a white foggy cloud mist, over the pond. I went over to the other side of the pond, at the edge of it. There were wild strawberries, just smiling red at me. I picked so many of them, that my fingers turned pinkish red. They were very small, and tasted as wild fresh strawberries. Just think of making a pie with the wild strawberries, this would be delicious.

A few steps down the road, I came to a wire fence, there were Alpine brown cows with a little gray color on them. The cows were closer to the middle of the field. I stood there a little while. The cows walked slowly to me, to greet me to say hello, in their own way. The cows had big eyes, and long eyelashes, it is like looking in their hearts. I walked away from the cows, and I said good bye.

The mountain country side, is so beautiful here with Alpine farm houses everywhere, and modern homes in their own part of their surroundings. Up here is beauty, that the Alpine mountain only holds. I am standing on the mountain, and I turned my head, to see on one side of myself, the beautiful clear lake, down below me, from the mountain. On the other side of myself, is more mountain that gets higher, and the mountain wants to touch the sky as I see. The tall trees, look like they get taller, when I look at the high part of the mountain. As I look up, and my body takes a breath, for I can breathe in, on the mountain that I can call, part of my home.

I walked down the road, a little bit more going towards the woods. I came to a fountain coming out of the ground, just having water coming out. Then I came to a small pasture, there were four cows, that had a wide leather strap around their neck, with a large bell, on the leather strap, and the large bell was hanging down. The bell rings every time the cows move, the cows were colored, black and white.

As I walked more, I came to some train tracks with beautiful stones next to them. There is a small old open air train, that can take me high up to the mountain, to a small mountain village. The old open air train, can also take me down the mountain to the shore of the beautiful clear mountain lake, or to a small lake front town.

I just stood here on the mountain, as I could see more of the bottom of the mountain, and the lake looking ever so beautiful. While I am standing here, and breathing the clear Alpine mountain air, I looked over to where the cows, were enjoying the fresh Alpine grass.

There is an old wooden farm, connected to a Chalet house, that is a Restaurant that serves, fresh homemade Alpine cheese fondue, with Alpine herbs, and Alpine mountain cheeses, this is their daily special. The Chalet house has a balcony, that is wooden, and carved very beautifully, and the Chalet house is very beautiful as it is built right on the side of the mountain, close to the ostentatious Castle that is built on the side of the mountain also.

I started to walk more, on the small road that went into the woods. I walked slow, so I could take in the beauty, and smell the clear clean fresh air. I see growing, right at the edge of the road, little bright Alpine blue flowers. They are so tiny, the little bright Alpine blue flowers, the blue color in the flowers, matches the color of the sky. The trees are very tall, and are all colors of greens, they have a look of polished. There was an enchanting feel I got as I walked, and the woods had me think, and I felt this is my home.

I heard a noise of water as I was walking, I came to a narrow stream, and the water was coming out of the ground, from the woods. The water had a clear look, and I see some white with the clear water, as the water moved over rocks, and passed green plants, growing next to the stream. For I did not want to leave here. Yet I never did, leave this place, it is forever in myself, I can see it, with my eyes, and my heart, for where I am, for where I go, it is all a part of who I am.

I got on the old open air train, and sat down. I took the old open air train up to the small village, on top of the mountain. Before I got there to the small village, as I was going up the mountain, the air got denser, because I was getting more in the woods, as the trees were right next to me, as I am in the train. I could just touch the leaves, from the plants growing, next to the train, as I am going passed. The air is so dense, it smells amazing. I am breathing the clean beautiful air now, as the train goes higher. I see woods, after woods, after woods, and Alpine homes carefully built by hand, so very cute, and beautiful hand carved wood, and the Alpine design that makes them unique. I see people working, outside on their farmland, as the train goes passed. I see more cows eating, wild Alpine grasses, and Alpine mountain flowers. How these magnificent beautiful Alpine cows walk, and stand on the sides of the mountains, is a good wonder to me. I am so high now, right on the top of the mountain, the very top. I get out of the old open air train. I start walking up the mountain a little, to the small village. As I am walking, there are two boys who are about college age. They started to talk French to me. I said some French, to them. Then I said I could speak, English to you, so we could talk better between us. We were talking, then it turned into that I sing, and I sang a song right here on top of the mountain, I started another song, then one of the boys sang with me, at this point. I am singing together with one boy, high on top of this mountain, and we sang great. When I was done singing the first song I sang, the boys said, I sang very good. That was very nice of them.

I start walking up, and it is getting higher as I am walking, this part of the mountain can be steep. It is perfect up here. For myself, the village, and the openness of standing high on top of this mountain, and high on top of the world, is perfect and beyond anything. Mountains have a world of their own, they are my world, and my whole being is here. I am sitting on a bench, looking down at the lake, with a clear perfect view. Being closer to the sun here, on top of this mountain clears the color of the lake, so the blues in the water shines even brighter, and my eyes just drink this all in.

I walk through the village, and pass fountains that stand by themselves, at different places in the village, and the fountains are made from mountain stones. Water flows out of the fountains all the time, and this is pure mountain water. When I pass by the fountains, I can take a drink, if it says I can, or I put my hands, under the flow of the water, and I feel cool mountain water, connecting to my skin. This is very healthy, and natural water, when I am drinking it, I taste the air, the woods and the mountain.

I walked down the mountain, just a little bit, and this part of the mountain is steep. I got to the old open air train, I went in and sat down. The train starts going down the mountain, and I am looking all around, I am up here, and I see in the distance, small towns far away, on the other mountains, I can see tall trees in the woods, and the breathtaking woods, only can be up here. I see farms, and farmland, and big manor homes. I love it up here, and there is peace here, and a life the mountain holds.

If cows are by the train track, I will see them. Cows are still eating here next to the train tracks, I seen them as I am coming down, and I see them as I go up the mountain, some cows look up at the train as it is going by, some just keep on eating. I am watching the cows, as I pass by. Birds fly up here, I am here too. I can take a breath, as the birds come to see what is up here too. I am coming to where, I can get off the train. This is the stop where the Castle is, I can see the Castle, through some parts of the trees. There is a mountain mist in the air. I am still on the mountain, and I get off the train, and I have a few steps to the ostentatious Castle.

I have had two of my Birthdays here, I ordered a cake from the bakery down the road, each time I had my Birthday here. Having my Birthday, when the cake arrived, I took a slice of, delicious cake that was made of yellow cream and chocolate cake, with chocolate curls on top. I know there was mountain water in the cake. I loved the cake, I gave some to my guests, and they wanted more, and I gave them more.

I am walking inside the Castle and I see a door is opened, and I look inside, the walls are ornately carved with gold. Wood beams on the ceiling are painted gold. This room is made for an Empress of Austria. Another room has a big fire place, when the fire is going, the room is warm, and cozy. The smell of the fire, on the wood as it is burning, smells of the woods from the outside, and freshness from Birch trees, Pine trees, Spruce trees in the room, and all throughout the Castle, it is very inviting. I am so very happy I am standing here.

Outside of the Castle, there is deep red colored roses, climbing on the walls. In another garden there are large size snails, feeding on anything, that they can find. Small wild Alpen flowers, dance around a bit, in the beautiful green grasses by the Castle. I look down from the window, at times, I can see the cows eating on the side of the mountain. Sometimes the window is open, and I can hear the cow bells, singing in the wind, beautifully.

I sing sometimes, in the Castle.

I stand in a home, that was once owned by an Empress of Austria, she wanted a Castle so she could be next to a lake, and a mountain. The Empress, had this one built for her. I feel her presence here, in this home, that was hers, and how grand she was. For myself, I make my own presence here, I feel as she once did.

I am here, and I give a royalness to myself.

This Castle, is all by itself, on the side of a mountain, and there are the woods, the cows, and places close by, and tall beautiful trees that have beauty written all over them. The unique beautiful colors of greens, of the plants growing, with the help and love of the majestic enchanted mountain, clean mountain air, and everything works together, for this magical growth.
With the mist on the mountain at times, that has myself, fall in love with this place.
I found home here.

# Chapter Twenty

## Orange Blossoms, and Myself

Both of my parents loved going to Florida. For this was their second home. I went so many times with them. I know Florida so very well. I know how, it was in the past.
Riding in the car, with the windows opened, I would smell, oranges in the air, and white blossoms of the orange trees, and the smell, felt so good. White Blossoms, come first on the tree, then the oranges. Orange trees, are beautiful with the oranges on the tree, and with the white blossoms on. Orange tree blossoms smell wonderful, a softness of fruit, and pure delight. There were acres, and acres of fields of orange trees, as I was riding in the car, on the road, orange trees were on each side of the road.
Looking at the new high rise apartments in Florida that were being built. My Father went up in an elevator, to look at them, how they were being built. I was with him, and my Mother. He said, this is something like friends of their apartment, they were going to move into. The friends of my parents, were friends that guided my Father, when he started his own business. I was in their new apartment in Florida, I was in their home also. My parent's friends, were very gentle people, and very nice.
I was in Florida with my parents, we went to a building, that sold condominiums and apartments that were going to be built. This building had models of how they were going to look like when they were finished, so you could buy one right away. My Father looked around, and talked a lot. The

building, I was standing in, only had orange tree groves growing all around it. I was young at that time.
Being very young, I would go to a movie, in an outdoor theater, there would be a big movie screen outside. People would come with their cars. They would park their cars, in front of the big movie screen that was outside. There was a metal box next to the car window, so I could hear what they would say in the movie. When I went with the family we brought pillows, I wanted to listen, and enjoy every part of it.
My Father went to a lot of Auctions, farm auctions, estate auctions but mostly farm auctions, he loved to go. He always brought a cane with him, so when he wanted to buy something, he could put up his cane to bid, for the item he wanted buy. I went with him to an Auction once. My Father had an Auction once, for things he wanted to sell.
I go to Auctions, anywhere in the world, were I am.
There was a moment in time, when I was young. My Mother had invited two young girls over to our house, they were there for just a day. The beautiful young girls were African-American. Both of the young girl's hair, was braided, and I asked if they could teach me how to braid hair. They said yes. Ever since they taught me how to braid hair, I have been braiding my hair ever since. I braid my hair, with a plain braid, or a French braid. I braid my hair, as they do in Austria or Switzerland. I was in these countries when I braided my hair, I Love it.

I once said to my Mother, do you still have a bracelet, from long ago, I described it to her. I came over to her house, so we both could look at it, and I always loved the bracelet. She went in her bedroom, and then she went in her closet, she reached up on her shelf, and got her old pink jewelry box. The jewelry box had a little gold line painted almost at

the edge of the box on top, and the gold line was painted
all along the top square of the jewelry box. For this made
the jewelry box more regal looking. My Mother opened her
jewelry box, and inside it had a small mirror, and a little
ballerina that had a little ballerina outfit on, the ballerina
danced to the music of the jewelry box, when the jewelry
box is turned on in the back with a key. I really think my
Mother, had this jewelry box ever since she was little, for
this I know. My Mother said I could look at the bracelet,
and I did, there were two bracelets that I loved because
they were old, and they were hers. I asked her if I could
have them, she said yes. Years later my Mother, gave me
her old pink jewelry box. My Mother said to me, how do I
remember the bracelet, from long ago. For I just do
remember a lot. She always thought, this was always
great, that I could always recall a lot of things, and know
about people, and places, and things of whatever kind.
She loved this, and I know I am great at it, I love this
myself too.
I told my Father I loved him very much all the time. When I
see him in his office, I said I love him loud enough, so most
of the people working there could hear me say it.
My Father liked to take naps, on the sofa, or on the floor
right next to my parent's fireplace, even if the fireplace was
not burning wood. The fireplace was made from big white
stones. When I came to give him a hug, after he took a
nap, it was a tight hug. I said I have to go; he would say I
do not want you to go. I miss him so, ever so lovingly.
I once said to my Mother, you could never give me enough
money, and this meant my love is strong.
I could never write; enough about how great my Parents
are. I just see myself in them. Myself having a Great Love
that I have now, and my parents who were so wonderful,
and this I have for myself and my life, that they are

completely by my side forever. I will forever, hold them both up, with the **Highest Honor.**

I was at Disneyland once, and I was at Disney World twice, I loved every part of it all. I was on an elevator, at Disney World when I was young, I seen an actor, that I saw on the television. I was so happy, I ran to tell my Mother, she was shopping in a store there.

# Chapter Twenty-One

## Genteel, and Distinguished my Mother

A woman who loved life, even more her own life. She was a woman that was happy, with a smile on her face, that could warm a heart. She had a glow on her face, and she was part Native American Indian, and proud she was, this is my Mother. She is very much alive to me. I carry her in my pocket, I have her in my life now. I am her flesh, and blood. She will Forever, be with me. She was my Mother, but we were as friends, and everything combined. She trusted me, one of her friends, told me this. She is, and was a strength for myself, and my life. I was a strength for her. But my strength was different than anyone she knew. I knew her longer, then even some of her friends. I had a quietness of strength, that can, and could be better, this was like hers. But as she was, we both could be more outgoing than anyone, and shine brighter. We were two different people, but we were blood togetherness. I miss my Mother every day. I have become all that I am, and like my parents, for this I can recall, almost everything. Now I can do for myself, and my parents, they are both in my pockets, and in my mind, and my heart, for this is even higher than the sky. I am the happiest person, knowing my parents, wanted me to have my dreams, my hearts desires, to be free to fly my heart, to the most greatest parts of the world. And every time I fly, in my world, I fly with them. For my parents both were rare, and pulchritudinous, and **Sophisticated**.
My Mother was a great human being.

The food I made for her was homemade, healthy in every way. She loved the food, and this but a smile on her face. She always felt great eating it. She loved coming over to eat.

When I was very little, the only doll I ever had, was a Barbie Doll, and it was one of the first ones that were made. My Mother would be working in the bushes around the house in town. I brought my doll to play with in the bushes, and there were flowers planted between the bushes. I did this to be close to my Mother, were she was at that time, and what she was doing. So I played with my Doll, and I could watch my Mother.

My Mother went through the hardest of times, but she came through it, because of who she was. She had my Father, and they both loved each other.

For myself they both, blossomed in themselves, and in their life, they both beamed outstandingly.

To this day, I do not like the pressures my parents had in their life, and the pressures people put on them.

For in my life, I walked away from it. I listened to my heart, soul, and mind, and I followed myself. I know my parents, walk with me now.

When my Mother got married, she wore a faux pearl tiara, on her head. Then the veil was attached to the pearl tiara, the veil flowed beautifully down the back of my Mother, and her wedding dress. The pearls were beautiful on my Mother, I seen her in pictures. I see the tiara, and I was holding it once, and seeing it first hand, the beauty that made her so beautiful.

My Mother gave me her wedding dress, it was cream satin, with light netting on the décolletage. Covered buttons beautifully down the back of her wedding dress, and her wedding dress flowed in the back on the floor, so beautifully and so elegantly.

My Mother was genteel and distinguished.

# Chapter Twenty-Two

## Blueberries Wild, and Strength of Love

I had an upbringing like if I was a **Royal**. I could not show much feelings, but I had a lot.
I had the new shoes of the very best design, shoes that were made from the highest quality, and what shoes I needed and wanted, to fit my feet. I had new clothes all the time, any clothes I wanted, and they were made from the highest quality, and design. I can recall the stores I walked in, many are not there any longer. My clothes were made so very well, and my clothes were beautiful, the designs were really perfect, I always looked pulchritudinous, and exquisite.
I went to Florida for two weeks at Easter time, every year. I would come back with a tan, and no one else had one.
I went to the cottage, the lake house, that was on the lake, I would go on the weekdays and weekends in the Summers, and at times in the Spring, and Fall and Winters. My Father had someone build two different houses, on the lake. I lived in the first lake house, on one part of the lake, then the first lake house was sold, and the second lake house was built on a different part of the lake, I liked them both.

I am walking from the Lake house, then I walk across the small road, to the woods. I pick **Blueberries wild** as many as I want. While I am bending over to pick the berries, I see the blueberry leaves are beautiful green. Picking the blueberries, I reached under, and on the side of the little blueberry bush, as I am picking, I hear a noise of bushes, being moved. I know bears love blueberries, I did not see a bear, at this moment. I picked so many blueberries my bowl is full. My hands are a light color blue, from the blueberries.

I know I am done picking now, my bowl cannot have no more berries in it. I walk back to the house, and made a crust and I put the crust in a pie pan, then I put the wild blueberries in the crust with some other ingredients. I shall open the oven door, and place this very gently in the oven, the pie will bake for a little while. I smell the pie in the air, wherever I am going in the house, next to the Lake. As I open the oven door, I see the wild blueberries bubbling, and I know it is done baking. I have a towel in my hand, and I gently take out the beautiful blueberry pie from the oven very carefully. The blue color in the pie, from the wild blueberries, matches the beautiful blue of the lake, that is close by where they are growing, and from the woods with its woody soil, and with the trees next to them, that gives them nutrients. I take a piece of the wild blueberry pie, and place it on a plate, the pie is a little warm. I take my fork to the piece of pie, and I have a bite. I am a very good baker, and to make a piece of art out of food, and my Mother did have a piece of this pie.

I tasted my wild blueberry pie, it had a woody, and wild, fresh bite. I used my Mothers recipe book, that she got from my Grandmother. I liked this recipe book, because of the Beautiful pictures on the cover. The pictures on the cover of this recipe book, is how the food is going to look like, after it is made.

I've stepped into my world when I was born, the way it was, and the way I live, and all that I am.

I recall when I was very young, my parents went away on trips for my Father's business, or for something else. One time I was at home with the babysitter or maid, or maybe this older lady was called the nanny, for I did not know what she was called. I had a bag of marbles, and I could not find them, I really knew she took them from me. I went to her, and I said in my little child's voice, give me my marbles back to me, or I will tell on you, when my Mother and Father comes home. I was so very little when this cute part of my life was, I love this.

I was born happy.

I have walked on mountains and hills, and I feel free and happy with the multitude I have walked. I see the top of the Alps, and the breathtaking beautiful towns, that are gently nestled so very peacefully next to the Alps, I have been closer to the sky here, and it felt beautiful, and exquisite for this is the place I belong.

One time and place, after I sang to a group of people, I was told I sang very good, right after this, I went to a mountain and I walked up this beautiful mountain. There were woods, covering the whole mountain. I walked to the top, I felt the clean air, and I felt the happiest ever, and if I am on a mountain, or I am on land, or in the Forest, I feel the same, the happiest ever.

For myself, I pick beauty to be in.

Seeing my incredible parents, with me and them both together, can and does make me the happiest daughter, and a person to myself, and for myself.

I am proud, and to this very day, I am their child, for myself the way of living in a world, real or dream.

Both of my parents if they would've known about this book, and the stories that I know, and recalled, they would be so very deeply proud of me, and happy for themselves.

I know my Mother would say to me, Barbara how do you
recall all of this. This is a saying she said, to me a lot. I
miss both my Father, and Mother, I really wish they were
standing right next to me now.
I was my Father's little girl, and he knew it, and I also knew
it.
I was my Mother's little girl, and we both really knew it. I
will, and forever be their little girl.
I grew up, and I am all that I was, and I am still to this very
moment, myself.
If I could, I would have my Father and my Mother back to
life again, at this very moment.

Dreams and Royalty, and Love Story
Perpetually, and enduringly love.
It is just the start, to touch the lights rays, to the
beginnings.

Standing Straight up,
Fresh air in front,
Start walking, take another step, then another step to the
story,
And as the wind blows, it caught the story.